CEOs PRAY TOO

31-DAYS TO BUILDING
YOUR BUSINESS GOD'S WAY

FOREWORD BY
BISHOP JONATHAN L. WOODS SR.

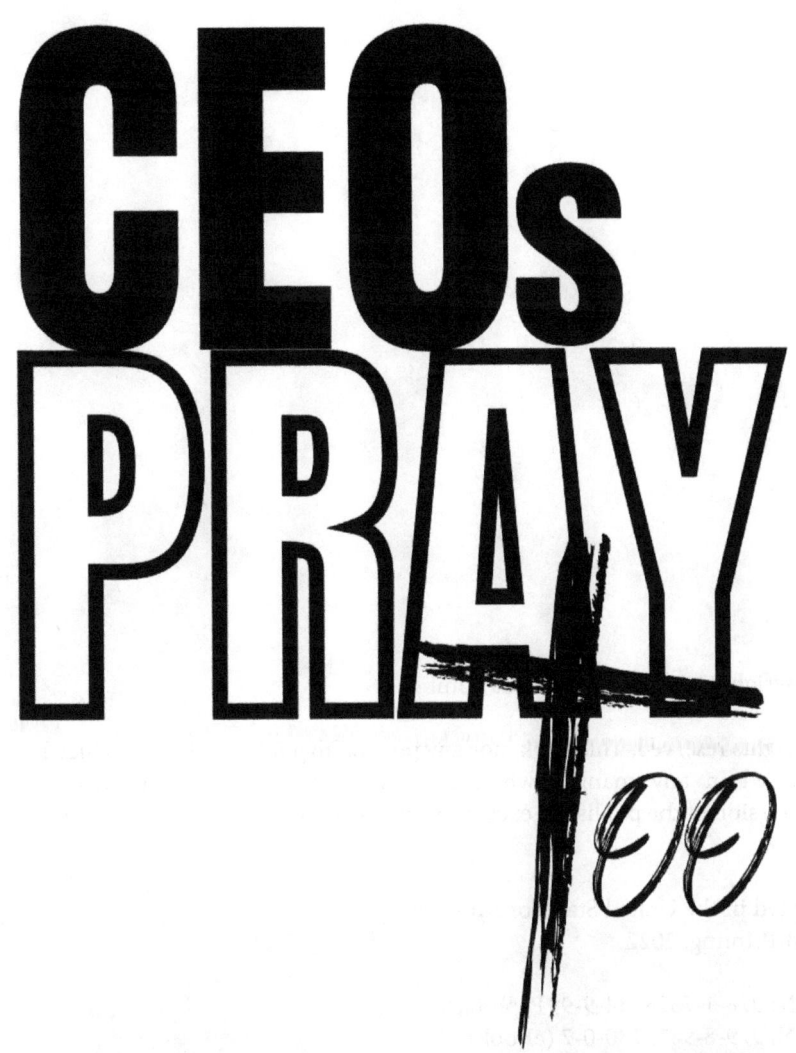

CEOs PRAY TOO

31-DAYS TO BUILDING
YOUR BUSINESS GOD'S WAY

DEE EDWARDS FOMBY

Copyright © 2022 Dee Edwards Fomby

All rights reserved. This book, nor any portion thereof, may be reproduced or used in any manner whatsoever without the expressed, written permission of the publisher, except for the use of brief quotations in a book review.

Printed in the United States of America
First Printing, 2022

ISBN: 978-1-7326434-9-9 (Paperback)
ISBN: 979-8-9873780-0-7 (eBook)
ISBN: 978-1-7326434-0-6 (Hardback)

Dee Edwards Fomby
459 Main Street #341
Trussville, AL 35173
dee@deeFomby.com

This book is dedicated to every marketplace and ministry leader, who desires to establish a mission and vision, using core values, based upon biblical principles and scriptures, to achieve great success in their business or ministry.

CONTENTS

FOREWORD......................ix
PREFACE.........................xi
Day 1............................ 1
Day 2............................ 5
Day 3............................ 9
Day 4............................ 13
Day 5............................ 17
Day 6............................ 21
Day 7............................ 25
Day 8............................ 29
Day 9............................ 33
Day 10........................... 37
Day 11........................... 39
Day 12........................... 43
Day 13........................... 47
Day 14........................... 51
Day 15........................... 55
Day 16........................... 59

Day 17	63
Day 18	67
Day 19	71
Day 20	73
Day 21	75
Day 22	77
Day 23	81
Day 24	83
Day 25	87
Day 26	91
Day 27	93
Day 28	97
Day 29	101
Day 30	103
Day 31	107
Prophetic Encouragement and Declarations	111

FOREWORD

For far too long, the world has seen faith and finances as two separate entities with no correlation. For many years, the image of the church world was that of believers being broke, struggling, miserable, and surviving by and by. For some, this image and the truth were a direct result of the lack of understanding that our life with God should be the catalyst for a better life for us here on earth. When practiced properly, the Christian faith should be the gateway to spiritual, mental, emotional, physical, and financial prosperity. To suggest that prosperity and spirituality are diametrically opposed is counterintuitive to God's heart for his creation. The Bible says in John 10:10, *"the thief cometh not, but for to steal, and to kill, and to destroy: I am come that they might have life, and that they might have it more abundantly."* These are the words of Jesus clearly explaining that his purpose for coming to the earth was to give all those that believed in him abundant life.

One of the sad realities of the church world is that we have emphasized the idea of eternal life, but we have neglected God's heart concerning abundant life. Eternal is for those who leave the earth, but abundant life is for followers of Jesus that are still on the earth. Children of God are supposed to be the real bosses. The inspiration to live a prosperous life should come from figures in the kingdom of God and not those in the kingdoms of the world.

When you study scripture, Abraham was rich, Job was rich, Solomon was rich, and this list just keeps going. This idea of God's people struggling is demonically inspired, and it has dramatically crept over into the four walls of the church. We must understand that as citizens of God's kingdom, we are supposed to be saved and paid, righteous and rich, faithful and favored. God's heart for his people is that the world will see the benefits of serving him through us, not just because of our morality but also because of our prosperity.

The life of a believer should be a testament to the power of God in every way.

Believers should have the best marriages, the best families, the best businesses, the best houses, the best cars, and ultimately the best of everything. This is achieved through a spiritual foundation connected with a progressive mindset.

In this 31-day business devotional, Dee Fomby will give insightful tools and strategies to be spiritually and financially successful in ministry and the marketplace. This devotion is guaranteed to upgrade the mindset of believers who have been vacillating with the idea of being saved and paid versus being saved and surviving. You will be positioned and set free from any negative thoughts seeded into you regarding the prosperity of God's people in ministry or marketplace. Get ready for your life to be changed as you read through this devotional.

Bishop Jonathan L. Woods, Sr
Senior Pastor
All Nations Church Fairfield

PREFACE

Headed For Destruction

Have you attended a conference, workshop, read books, followed the models of other entrepreneurs, watched videos, or read articles and your business or ministry still isn't thriving? Somewhere in the process, you're probably wondering if all the sacrifices that you have made are really worth it. Deep down you know that you have come too far to quit and have invested too much to give up now, but you feel stuck. And God won't let you walk away, even if you wanted to. That was me. I was depleted, drained, and desperate for a breakthrough in my business, but I wasn't quite ready to give up. I was missing something that would bring all the pieces together. I had the ideas, but no guidance or real plan for success.

Imagine, in your broken state of mind and with lean pockets, being totally sold out to God, serving in ministry, and nothing appears to work favorably for you. And on the other hand, seeing people with no Godly practices or integrity, excelling financially, and living the life that you desire. The world seems to have a system that produces quicker results than serving God does, and now you're being torn between two options: to follow the world's way or to allow patience to work in your life to yield the fruit and results of God.

Looking around in this digital world, it may feel as if you have to become like others, do what they do, or follow their way in order to obtain what they have. They must be doing something right. Now, the enemy is pointing out all the reasons why you need to abandon God's way and follow the standards of the world. IT'S A TRICK.

The blueprint for success is mainly the same for any business or ministry venture, but your success will be determined by what you believe, what you know, what you do, and whom you trust. You're one decision away from either obtaining instant gratification through trusting in the proof of what you see today or waiting for the manifestation of what will come to pass if you continue to stand with God.

There is always a quicker and easier way than the process necessary for what God wants to do in you. You can get what you want today, avoid the necessary process, and suffer the consequences, or take a journey with God that may take longer, and cause hardship and suffering. What does hardship and suffering produce in your life? An eternal glory that outweighs light and momentary troubles. It produces stability and sustainability. A lifetime of success, not just spouts of success. He wants your entire life to be successful. David had great success in everything he did because the Lord was with him. Even when he was being attacked, God still gave him success. When he became an adulterer and murderer, God was still with him. You need the Lord to be with you at all times.

Contrary to what you may have heard, you can have a life of success, but If you submit and trust God to start in faith, and then down the line remove Him, you will never reach your maximum potential. God wants you to have it all. Saul was anointed by God, but along his journey, he quit obeying Him due to the pressure of life and people. He acted hastily, trying to obtain something that already belonged to him, instead of waiting and obeying. This is the problem with living in a microwaveable world: we don't want to wait; we want it now.

Like other faith-based business and ministry leaders, you may have started your journey on the right track, but how you respond when you start experiencing decline, or the unexpected happens, is important. Oftentimes, people go into panic mode and revert to old practices, philosophies, and hustles that don't align with who they currently are. I was a hustler on the street, and I thought that same mindset was going to sustain me as a business owner. Little did I know that would be the beginning of my downfall.

I went from being sought out and experiencing massive success in my business to almost a 50 percent loss of income. I was fighting to hold on to my clients and fighting to keep my lifestyle while spending less time aligning with God's Word. It was like nothing that I did worked. I was unknowingly out of alignment with God, because I was busy doing things my way, and I didn't realize it until it was almost too late. The Bible says there is a way that seems right unto man but the end results will produce destruction, and I was headed full speed ahead on the path of destruction.

I fell into the trap of the enemy by recklessly pursuing my own desires. I wanted it when I wanted it and how I wanted it. I was in survival mode. I stopped obeying and seeking God. Missing one day with God turned into two days and then three days. Before I knew it, I was talking to Him while I was on the run while working overtime trying to get my business to become what He told me it could be. By the time I noticed the direction my business was taking, I was losing clients and money. Everything was leaving faster than it was coming in. I was at a standstill: in desperate need of a change, or I would be heading back to regular employment. What was happening in my life?

God was allowing my process to strip me down so that I could see how much I really needed him. It was a setup, but I didn't know it. I thought it was the enemy, but it was me. It was my choices and decisions that led me to become dry, drained, and desolate. What I finally realized through the ups and downs of business is that God cared more about me, than He did the business. He still does.

He Threw The Final Blow

I am God's priority; I am His vision and His Word. He stands over us and watches His Word, making sure we fulfill what we were sent on the earth to do. Any good parent isn't going to stand around, doing nothing, while the kids aren't obeying, listening, and are being led astray. Instead, they may have to take extreme measures to get their attention, such as rebuke, chastisement, punishment, or taking the TV away. Usually, parents will take away something that they love to get them back on track and focused. There are times that God may have to stand back and watch over you while you make whatever decision you're going to make, then give you grace when you fall.

My husband, Jeremiah David, had received many warnings from God. He would ride the train of grace and go back to doing the same thing. Then one day, his actions left him with a broken back, on a walker, and unable to take care of himself. He wasn't sure if he was ever going to walk again. Many people who have broken their L4 vertebrae end up paralyzed… wheelchair bound. God had to throw the final blow.

This is what God had to do to me: let me lose clients, experience embarrassment, and once everything was stripped away, I had no other choice but to turn to the real CEO of my life. Every loss that I have experienced in my life served a great purpose. It was necessary for my growth and development and led me right back to Him.

According to **James 1:6-8,** *"Be very glad, there is wonderful joy ahead, even though you must endure many trials for a little while. These trials will show that your faith is genuine. It is being tested as fire tests and purifies gold - though your faith is more precious than mere gold. So when your faith remains strong through many trials, it will bring you much praise and honor..."* I had to show God that I was ready for elevation. He had to break me down to build me back up. He had to slow me down to teach me His ways: to teach me how to obey even when I didn't understand. I was so used to things happening quickly in my life... I have been on my own since I was 16 years old; all I knew was the fast life, and when things didn't go my way, I knew how to go into survival mode.

You Had to Go Down

You may have to go through many trials and tribulations, but when you make it through the valley be prepared to receive your reward. Initially, I didn't fully understand that the tests and the storms were helping me to discover my purpose. It was the suffering that was maturing me. I had to hit rock bottom. I thank God for where I have been, and I appreciate where I am today. God had to slow me down, and during this process, I had to examine myself. I was the common denominator to everything that was going wrong in my life. I wanted more out of life, but it seemed like I couldn't recognize who I was, or how I had gotten to this place.

I was different from Jesus. When Jesus was led into the wilderness and tempted for 40 days, he resisted. I wasn't able to resist what the enemy was telling me that he could give me. God was trying to lessen the suffering, but I wanted what I could see now, instead of waiting on what He promised me. It was surely going to come to pass. I was going to have it. I was going to have the influence, houses, cars, and money, but God wanted to make sure I had my soul. I felt like my motives were right, but I was doing it the wrong way. It was like the devil was promising me the same vision that God was going to give me. Did you catch that? The devil was promising me, which means that he wasn't going to give it to me. He was mocking God. He was using the right words and the right vision to lead me astray. God was going to give it to me, but He wanted to be the link that brought it all together. That's when God spoke to me, through Amos 3:3, **"How can two walk together unless they agree?"** I was moving ahead of God by forcing pieces together. I was trying to do it my way. It was like two people being chained together going in different directions. God was going in one direction, and I was going the other way until eventually, the chain broke, and I lost access like Adam and Eve.

God allowed me to be in a position of what seemed like a failure or a "holding place," just to get me back on track like Jonah. God had given Jonah an assignment that he did not want to complete, so God had to put him in the belly of a whale; what I consider a holding place. On the outside, it looked as if I was winning, but I was struggling just like the next person trying to make it day-to-day. There were things that I knew I was supposed to be doing, things that dropped in my spirit regarding my business but ignored it. I didn't obey. It seemed too complicated to do it His way, so I turned a deaf ear, and His voice became unrecognizable concerning my business until I found myself drowning in sorrow and debt. That's when God stepped in; He intervened to show me the way - His way. This was the moment I was introduced to the new Chief CEO of my life: God.

New Beginning and A Fresh Start Await You

Imagine the Garden of Eden as the business. God created the heavens and earth, then gave Adam, one of the greatest entrepreneurs to walk the earth, consent to name every animal. Like Adam, God has employed you to use your authority and abilities to build your business or ministry. Your ministry is your business. You are equipped with every tool to run it well. You have everything that you need right now, including a partner to help you when you are tired, drained, and unsure of your next move: the Holy Spirit. However, your motivation to carry out God's will should not precede His voice. The moment Adam disobeyed God, he lost his company, and one decision affected everything in the garden.

You are employed by God to become a physical representation of Him on earth in order to carry out His business plans. That's why scripture says that we shall do greater works than His Son. On the sixth day, God declared, *"It is finished."* His work was done, then He passed the torch to believers in seven mountains of influence: business, government, media, religion, arts and entertainment, education, and family. Every believer has been given authority to operate, dominate, and rule in at least one of these spheres of influence with the gifts and abilities needed to carry on His works until the day of His return. Therefore, your work isn't finished yet.

You Have Work to Do

As a marketplace leader, your business is a tool God has given you to serve Him and His people. He provides you with resources so that you can give to others. He opens doors for you so that you can open them for others. He grants you favor so that you can extend favor to others. What God has done for you, you are responsible for doing for others. God wants to trust you with success, wealth, and a sustainable business and ministry. He has granted you access and has given you permission to be His voice and vessel on earth, but can you be trusted?

God trusted Adam and made him a business owner. He gave him instructions not to eat from the tree of the knowledge of good and evil. He established boundaries- a business plan- in the beginning, so there would be no excuses, then he left Adam to run his business as he saw fit. Whatever Adam said, God obliged. They had access to everything in the garden, including the tree, but they didn't have permission or the authority to eat from it. God will tell you "no," to keep your flesh disciplined because you need to know that everything is not beneficial, even if you have access to it. When boundaries were crossed, God held Adam responsible for Eve's actions. He was reprimanded when she didn't obey because she was under his leadership. In other words, she was employed by Adam, and Adam was employed by God. Adam was found guilty because he was left in charge.

It's like passing a baton in a race. God passed it to Adam; that's why He didn't go directly to Eve. The command was given to Adam, and he became liable for everybody in his business. Adam stood there and heard the conversation between the serpent and Eve. He even watched her eat the fruit, and instead of him correcting her, he ate it too. What would have happened if God saw that Adam was willing to lead his team (wife) by correcting her when she disobeyed the instructions? Could it be possible they were kicked out of the garden because there was no accountability from the leadership? Leaders are held to a higher standard than the people they lead. When the team goes astray, it's not their fault; it falls back on the leadership. When you stop following God's way, and you allow others under your leadership to disobey without correction, it can lead to a great fall for you and your company. You are ultimately liable, and that's why it is important to trust and obey God.

The Formula of Success

Through my failures, disappointments, and setbacks, God has taught me to seek Him in three areas: wisdom, knowledge, and understanding. When you have these three traits, you'll have the solution to all your struggles in life. He said, "if anyone lacks wisdom, ask and I will give it to you liberally." In other words, if you don't know what to do or how to handle a situation, He wants to provide you with the answers. He's your Business & Life Coach. You never have problems He can't solve; instead, you don't have enough wisdom, knowledge or understanding, or a combination thereof to resolve the problem on your own. I've learned that everything that I need can be found in Him, and when I discovered this formula for success, I found that He is the number one key to success. He is a Wonderful Counselor. Although I had to start all over, this time, I made sure that God was appointed as the CEO of my life. My commitment is to Him first, and everything else falls under His umbrella.

You Have Been Challenged

I challenge you to devote the next 31 days of your life to read this daily devotional and allow it to guide you into prayer and meditation regarding different areas of your business or ministry. You'll find this book to be very helpful as I discuss scriptures that will assist you with ministry and marketplace. Let me be the one to say that you've done well getting to this place; now it's time to go higher. There's another level that will yield greater fruit than you have ever seen.

The best thing to ever happen to me was when my life fell apart - completely out of my hand, in order for me to lean upon His everlasting arms. If you're struggling in any area of your business, ministry, or life, your answer is in God's Word. You'll be amazed at all the knowledge that is found in scripture for ministry and marketplace leaders. God has always understood the role of a business leader: how to delegate, build a team and create several streams of income because He did it first.

Whether you're excelling or failing, you are in a perfect place to seek God's Word concerning the advancement of your business or ministry. This daily devotional will guide you into the truth regarding you as an entrepreneur and ministry leader. I encourage you to take notes, meditate, pray, and apply. Ask God to open your heart to receive prophetic revelation from reading each day. Some days you will feel as if you are on the right track; other days, you will feel as if you have missed the mark. Either way, there is a solution found in God's Word. If I found the answers to business success in Him, I know you will as well. Let this be the start of a brand new life, and let me be the first to say Happy Birthday. Welcome to your new beginnings and your new life of success.

Leaders to Entrepreneurs,

Dee Fomby

Dee Fomby

Day 1

Matthew 6:34 - "Give your entire attention to what God is doing right now, and don't get worked up about what may or may not happen tomorrow. God will help you deal with whatever hard things come up when the time comes."

As an entrepreneur, it is easy to get worked up, stressed out, and overwhelmed thinking about finances, sales, clients, products, employees, services, bills, family, and friends. On top of the uncertainty regarding the trouble that tomorrow may bring, life can leave you feeling mentally drained: up one minute and down the next. No matter how bad things may appear to be, take control of your life and learn to live in the moment. Live in your now. Control the things that you can by making the necessary adjustments to lead with a positive attitude. Negativity clouds your ability to see a solution or a way out. It's one of the silent tactics of the enemy to plant seeds of discord between what God said and what you see. That's why the moment you start doubting yourself, it is important to guard your five senses: sight, sound, taste, smell, and touch. This is how the body receives information. When they are unprotected and exposed, the enemy uses something as small as reading a social media post to get you off course, waste your time, or plant seeds of doubt. It is his job to deceive you and make small things appear to be larger than life. He is the father of lies, but you can control your thoughts by literally speaking against the negative seed. When the enemy tells you that you're incompetent, your response should be, "according to the Word, God calls me a conqueror and an overcomer." Speak life. Cancel those statements with the truth of God's Word, even if you don't believe it at the time, so He can help you deal with whatever hardship is thrown your way.

As a CEO, you'll always be faced with challenges, but you are called to handle them, even when you don't feel like you are best suited. What can you do to face the problems head-on? What do you need to put in place to get the results you desire? It's okay if you don't know right now. Your first response is to step back and breathe. Release anxiety and fear. Relax. Now invite God into your situation so that you can hear His solutions. You can not make Godly decisions when you are frustrated; instead, your emotions will lead you to make fixed decisions based on temporary situations. When you are stressed and feel like running from situations, check the baggage and burdens that you are carrying. Do they belong to you, or do they belong to others? What can you do to minimize your load? Answer those questions, then give your entire attention to what God is doing right now - not tomorrow or the next day. Right now.

The pessimistic outlook of the Israelites kept them in the wilderness for a long time because they were focused on what they couldn't see. When things weren't going according to plan, they questioned everything that they once had full confidence in, including their leadership. They had forgotten it was God who led them to this place and provided their every need. They were too blind to see where they were going. They were a short distance from the promised land, but negativity and complaining kept them in Egypt much longer.

If God fixed a situation in your business or ministry before, then have full confidence and unwavering faith that God will help you to deal with whatever hardship that comes your way. Receive strength and wisdom to handle what you feel you can't. You are equipped and qualified to handle the ups and downs of being a CEO. Enjoy your journey of success. Your performance, creativity, and results are more favorable when your mindset is stable and secure. Hardship is part of the process that makes you a better CEO. It was never intended to break you but to teach you how to lean not to your own understanding but in all your ways, acknowledge Him, and He will direct your path. It may hurt now, but wisdom is matured through trials and tribulations. God is your source, solution, and support. As long as He is with you, the outcome will always be favorable toward you.

Prayer: Father, when I feel overwhelmed and stressed, thank you for intervening and reminding me that you are my way, my truth, and my light. You are a burden lifter and carrier. I invite you into my business and ministry to help me make decisions that glorify you. Help me to rely upon your wisdom in times of trouble. You are my way of escape. Show me how to deal with the hardships that will come my way. Help me to concentrate on today and the promises that you have already predestined for this day in Jesus' name. Amen.

Day 2

> *Romans 8:28, "And we know that God causes everything to work together for the good of those who love God and are called according to his purpose for them."*

How many times has God delayed traffic to keep you from being involved in a car accident? Or maybe your heart has been broken by a dear friend only later to discover that person really didn't like you? Or the business deal that you wanted didn't work out because God had a better one in store for you? I remember the days when I felt all alone in our business. There were times that I wanted to break down. Walk away. But even in those times, God has always proven Himself to us. Life happens whether we want it to or not. You can do everything right and still harvest a bad result because everything that happens in your life is tied to your purpose. Many things that you thought you weren't going to be able to handle, you survived because of what's inside of you. God will never allow anything to come upon you or place you in situations that you are not equipped to handle. He knows you're victorious. He knows you can really handle it. He knows more about you than you know about yourself, and when you are faced with trials and tribulations, they bring you into the full knowledge of God and you. Sometimes, it's not until we go through the valley that we realize who we are. God loves you so much that when you are weak, His power is made strong in your life. He is saying that in your weakest moment, He will carry you even when you feel that you can't go on. When you are overwhelmed, He has a plan. He needs you to know that you serve a well-able God. He wants you to know your own strength and your abilities. You are built for this.

In order for you to reach your full potential, things won't always work out according to plan. You will be faced with many disappointments and what appear to be setbacks in your business, but they are speed bumps to help you slow down and see the full view more clearly. Imagine traveling down a road, and then you notice a speed bump ahead. As you approach the speed bump, you may take a glance around and notice the children playing nearby, or the mail carrier who stopped suddenly ahead, or even the dog that ran out in the middle of the road. You would not have been able to see those things if you hadn't slowed down to approach the speed bump. Now imagine the speed bumps that you are facing in your business: sales are down, and employees are calling in. You didn't close the deal, profits margins are low, overhead is high, and you feel as if you're in a rut. Stand back. Take a break. Reflect on God's Word, and don't make a drastic decision. When the Word of God is rooted in your heart, Heaven and Earth may fade away, but God's Word shall remain. It shall manifest. You have to believe it during moments of difficulty and frustration. His Word will be your reassurance that what's been against you is going to work somehow in your favor. When you take the time to seek GOD before moving forward, He will give you an impression or even a thought that will provide you with the answer you need. It may not come at that moment, but I can guarantee you that it will be on time. You just have to learn not to panic.

Oftentimes the most difficult part of seeing it all come together is waiting patiently. It seems as if it is taking God forever to move obstacles out of the way or even shed light on a situation. That's the time that God wants you to have all your trust in Him. The vision is for an appointed time. You can never go wrong when you follow God. You just have to be willing to obey His word. You have a promise that's attached to every challenge you may be facing. God promises that it is going to work out for the good of those who love the Lord. You have to keep loving God. You have to continue to walk in your purpose even when the devil is trying to distort your view of God. His tactic is to kill your faith because it's impossible to please God without it. Therefore, the enemy wants to snatch it away. He doesn't want it to grow. Without faith, you will become stagnant, and you will not experience the full abundance of God in your life or be able to produce good deeds.

The truth of the matter is that when the heat is intensified and when things happen in our life that is out of our control, God is either purging things and people who have become a hindrance to your growth, preparing you for the next level, or allowing your faith to be tested. This comes right before elevation. Put all your trust in God, and don't change course. Stay on the path. Keep doing what you were doing until you hear God say to move or to do something differently. Trust the Holy Spirit as He directs your path.

As a leader, you'll carry the most weight and experience the most trials, letdowns, and disappointments in order for God to open your eyes to what you couldn't see when things were moving full speed ahead. Life is a process. Life is your teacher. It's always going to be one thing after another so that you can grow, mature, and learn to trust God every step of the way. If you allow what you are experiencing to have its perfect work in you, then you are going to come out of this lacking nothing. The pieces will come together.

Prayer: Father, I thank you for guiding me into truth. I may not like or even understand why certain things had to happen in my life or business. I don't like the pain, loneliness or the sadness that I sometimes feel, but I trust that you are using my suffering and disappointments for your good. When I don't see a way, help me to turn to you as my way, truth, and light. I trust that you see and you know all. Help my unbelief. Thank you for using me and trusting me to be an ambassador for you in my business and ministry in Jesus' name. Amen.

Day 3

Matthew 7:7, "Ask and it will be given to you; seek, and you will find; knock, and it will be opened to you."

Do you have an issue with asking for what you need? Is your issue with asking particular people? Do you feel as if you're begging when you ask others for something? The most vulnerable position that leaders can ever be placed in is feeling as if they're begging people to complete a task, especially those you pay and sacrifice the most for. It takes confidence to place yourself in a position to be denied, rejected, and let down because people will not always respond the way we want them to. These are true emotions that are conjured up when either asking someone to do something they have already declined to do or asking them again when they haven't yet responded.

Many times when things don't go our way, we either become discouraged, decide to take things into our own hands, get an attitude, or give up. When the key to your success is seeking out a positive way to overcome the objection. The solution is persistence. Asking, seeking, and knocking continuously until the door is open sometimes seems foolish to others, but this is how you become persistent and get what you want.

Persistence is a desirable characteristic that many people would love to have, but many lack the confidence to pursue it. Having the nerve and the guts to ask an individual for something repeatedly seems very assertive and aggressive, but it really shows how badly you desire the outcome to work in your favor. In the business world, this is known as sales. Being able to hear a "no" over and over again until that one person says, "yes," only to do it all over again. The truth of the matter is that as a leader, people are not going to respond when and how you desire all of the time. They may not even want to do it for you. But your persistence and a positive attitude can cause people who don't even like you to bless you.

As a CEO, it's not about whether or not people like you. From time to time, you may feel as if you are begging God or even pleading for people to hear your request or respond to your needs. But you can't give up just because things don't go your way. No matter how many doors close, or how many people say no, if you are after a, "Yes," seek it! Don't take no for an answer.

Many times people don't want to say no, but they do because they don't have enough information to make an informed decision. Just like a salesperson, they are trained in their mind to say no, but the more information you provide and match it with their desire, need, or reason - their no will eventually become a yes, now or later. Explain in detail and provide more insight to help the person be open to your request. Also, it's a great idea to listen to them first and then ask questions. The information you gathered will show them the benefit(s) of saying yes to you based upon what they said. Use what they said to help persuade them.

It's easy to throw a title, position, and social status around to influence people into saying yes; however, people will appreciate and respect who you are and what you do when you take the time to help them to feel at ease about your request. It's called building rapport. You know the end result you are trying to achieve, but the way you start makes all the difference in the world. Getting to that place is going to take asking, seeking, and a whole lot of patience, which is one of the greatest gifts God has given us, even if we don't use it.

God is very tolerant and gives us free will to choose. God wants us to agree with Him, and each time we make a request, our motives and intentions are being tested. God is seeking full alignment. He is after your yes like you are after the yes in a sales call. He wants you to put aside what you desire and seek Him first. Seek His will, even in business. God will cause your enemies to say yes to you when you have a yes from Him. The problem is that we are seeking people first and God last. Are you asking, seeking, and knocking with an intent to bring glory to Him? If you are, God promised that every door will be opened unto you, and it will make selling easier.

Prayer: Father, help me to seek after you in all that I do. Sometimes I move too fast and want things to go my way. However, I realize today that a Yes from you means a yes in my life even when doors close. Help me not to lose focus of who you are to me; and how important it is for me to ask you first. I desire to seek after your will; then I know that every door will be opened unto me in Jesus' name. Amen.

Day 4

James 2:26, "Faith without works is dead."

Oftentimes, we start in faith, then somewhere in the process, we tend to rely upon our own abilities and talents to take us higher. That's actually not the problem. The problem is when we believe more in what God has given us than we do in God. The abilities that God has given you can make it easy and dangerous at the same time to rely upon God. The dangerous part is having the anointing without the presence of God. This is why anointed people can experience some of the greatest downfalls. When the Lord departed from Saul, he was still leading and operating in position, but the Lord was not with him. You will be able to tell by the fruit of a person's life whether God is with them because faith will always produce good works.

What is works? It's a faith activity that produces results. The scripture states that faith by itself is useless, so you have to partner faith with action to produce results.

What does works look like? Works usually will cause you to move outside of your abilities. When there is no faith, you can move but produce no fruit: fruitless actions. Faith is your connection to God, and it is a tool used to move you into purpose. It is your ability to move forward without having all of the answers. It is the instrument that is used to stay ahead of your competitors and drive success within every component of your business and ministry. Faith moves will always promote you above others. It is the ingredient that makes all the pieces come together. Faith tells you to do what doesn't logically make sense to others to reveal the substance.

According to **Hebrews 11:1 - Now faith is the substance of things hoped for, the evidence of things not seen.** As a leader, when you start a project or hire teammates, you don't have any proof that what you see by faith will actually work. Faith gives you confidence so that while you may not know how it is going to happen, when it is going to happen or how much time it is going to take for it to happen, you know that it will happen. And even if it doesn't, faith tells you that God willed the outcome to happen the way He wanted it to happen. Faith gives you the ability to trust God with the outcome.

Keep your faith in motion; the people you lead need to see your faith on display. Think, prepare, and execute your next move. Ask God to make you a forward thinker. This way, you can stay innovative and in front of your competitors and your team. Write the vision down and make it plain, so they can run with your current goals while you are working on your next move with God. It's your ability to trust in what you know but don't see.

Something will always happen that attempts to throw you off course, but safeguard your faith and do not allow it to shift in reverse. The fruit of doubt is inconsistency, lack, bondage, fear, and poverty.

In order for faith to move you in the right direction, just know that things are going to happen out of the blue. God uses the unexpected in your life to propel you forward. Therefore expect roadblocks to happen. Welcome them and learn to work through the mishaps. Roadblocks are there to make you prove how bad you want what's on the other side, and when you knock them down by being persistent, consistent, and immovable, you'll see that you were only a wall away from the blessings that await you on the other side.

One of my teammates experienced one of the most trying seasons in her business: betrayal. By the time she showed up for an interview, she had disconnected from people and didn't believe in the honesty of small business owners. I laugh now as I think back on it. She was supposed to be convincing me she was the right person for the position, but I spent my time convincing her that I was the right person for her life. Faith caused her to walk through the door for what she thought was only a position, but God had a breakthrough waiting on the other side of the wall. Faith moved her forward. God used her faith to enter into the tax industry after spending years as a licensed cosmetologist, and he used faith to heal her. She is a demonstration of what happens when faith takes the wheel.

When one door closes, another door is ready to open. Position yourself to take on new opportunities or create new ones when one door closes. When you feel that your faith is drowning in doubt, ask God to help your unbelief. Start working again as if the vision was just planted in your heart. Work in faith and keep your eyes on God. Address any problems with grace and wisdom, but keep focusing on the promise.

Prayer: Father, I thank you for giving me faith that drowns out my doubt. My faith is leading me to consistently work hard and smart in my business because I am a Kingdom-driven entrepreneur. Thank you, Lord, for trusting me and giving me the faith to start and finish in faith. My words will produce good deeds in Jesus' name. Amen.

Day 5

Habakkuk 2:2 - "Write the vision; make it plain on tablets, so he may run who reads it."

In a relay race, when a runner finishes one leg of the race, he is required to pass the baton to the next runner to give him permission to start the next leg of the race. This is an example of what your written plan does for you and others on your team. It provides permission, direction, and guidance. Without this plan, you do not have a solid foundation to build, which leads to confusion, employee turnover, frustration, and business loss. Leaders who don't have a written plan do not have a clear view of the end results. Written documentation causes you to think deeper and more intensely. It helps to track goals and becomes a guide to stay on course like a GPS. It's a handbook of expectations for your future teammates. Even if you're the only one on your team right now, build your business as if you have an entire team. As the leader, you must first understand the direction of the business or ministry. Vision clarity is important. The more understanding you have as to what you are building, the more you will be able to communicate it to others.

In the race, the participants are usually given a map of the course. They review it before the race. They memorize it, and they can see obstacles on the trail because of what is written. When you listen and submit to the Holy Spirit, you will not be caught off guard. God will forewarn you about things to come. The Bible declares that nothing will happen on earth unless He first reveals it to his prophets. As the CEO, you are the prophet for your business and ministry. God will give you instructions, revelation, knowledge, and insight. You'll know the sustainability of your company. You will stay ahead of the trends because He is the one that will revise the plan to guarantee success. Delay won't be your portion!

Delays are often a result of a lack of faith or guidance, which usually derives from a vision that isn't plain enough for others to run with. Clear vision should answer how, what, when, where, and who. If you are wearing multiple hats or you are the only person in the business or ministry, you are one body, but you are actually many members. What does this mean? It means that you have a team on the inside of you that you must give the vision to until someone comes and occupies that role. Don't be dismayed. Run the race with endurance until others catch hold of the vision. Get more clarity even if you have to go to God over and over again until the vision is clearly written on the tablets of your heart. He's your partner. Moses had to go to the mountain twice to receive the Ten Commandments. **VISIT GOD AGAIN!**

Can you imagine running a race in the wrong direction? Or some of the runners running in the opposite direction, making the wrong turn, quitting out of frustration, or not running at all? Chaos! Complete disorder and confusion. A lack of knowledge will never produce finishers, just failures, quitters, and complainers because they don't have a vision to refer back to. It's like driving a car backward on the interstate when you don't have a written plan; accidents that you could have avoided will surely happen. Write the vision.

A plan is your vision written out. It is your book of knowledge. It's like a Bible to your company. It is your guide. It is a contract. It helps you to stay on course. When you're lost or discouraged, it's where you reference to see what is written. It's your hope and your future. It houses the mission and vision statement. It's your memory. Discuss the vision everywhere you go. As frequently as we see the Nike sign or we know the slogan for Chick-Fil-A, get it into the hearts of people all over the world. Post it everywhere. Say it often. Read it frequently. Visualize it. Let others run with your vision after death. Can they carry it on?

How many times have foundations been created on behalf of those who are deceased? Many of the books we read today from deceased authors are still active and live because the vision was made plain. Martin Luther King Jr. had a clear vision that we still honor today. May your vision be carried out beyond your existence on earth.

Prayer: God, help me to write the vision plain. Father, help me to spend time seeking you for visual clarity so that I can easily give instructions to others to carry out your plan. Forgive me when I've rushed the process or become impatient because of the pressure I am experiencing around me. Help me to understand that the more I seek you, the more clarity and understanding I receive from you. May your plan become my plan in Jesus' name. Amen

Day 6

Proverbs 29:18, "If people can't see what God is doing, they stumble all over themselves; but when they attend to what he reveals, they are most blessed."

Imagine having a bow and arrow ready to launch, but you don't have a target. Can you still shoot? Yes, but you will be shooting aimlessly. You may be a trained, skilled archer, but without a target, it will become hard to measure your skills. And in the same way, if you don't have an objective, you will not be able to measure the success you desire. You will soon stumble over the vision and lack the reassurance that is necessary to reduce stress and anxiety.

Leaders must have specific and measurable goals to understand the direction of their business or ministry. This is how you measure growth and engagement by the goals you set. You have to be able to use data, something tangible, to see what God is doing. I was in a service one day, and Apostle Ryan Lestrange said, "there is someone who can't hear out of their left ear." When the young lady went to the altar and he laid hands on her and began speaking the word of the Lord. The Lord healed her instantly, and she was able to hear in that moment. There was evidence of what God said.

What you hear and what He says should coincide, and then you will have tangible evidence in your ministry and business that God is with you as long as you move accordingly. How long do you think you will be able to go to the gym if there weren't any results? Not long.

Anything God is in should always be producing fruits and progressing. God moves forward, and he makes big. The Bible says that when Jesus taught, crowds would come from near and far, and the church grew daily. They were able to see, and have evidence of the work that Jesus did. When you tend to what God reveals, what you do will be blessed. There is a story in the Bible where God told Lot to take his family, move out of the city, and don't look back. Lot's wife looked back, and she turned into a pillar of salt. I don't know the reason she looked back, but I can imagine that she was probably reminiscing or mourning over her home, her responsibilities, and other family members and friends she had to leave behind in order to move forward. God had to separate them in order to progress them. There are some people you can't grow with. There will be times when God is trying to elevate you, and He has to pull you from your place of comfort in order to push you closer to your destiny. The higher you climb, your obedience will disconnect those who aren't ready to go with you. Progression sometimes means separation.

Along this journey, you may not understand why He chooses a particular route but trusts the process. He will reveal signs along the way to confirm that you're headed in the right direction. These signs are your validation and proof that you are on the right path. Life can happen so suddenly that we tend to forget what He has done. Therefore, take an inventory of your blessings. Try counting them so that you can stay hopeful and grateful about where He has called you to go so you do not stumble. It's like a marriage; if you concentrate on the bad moments, the relationship will fail, but if you are attentive to the things that have gone well despite obstacles, you will be rewarded. Open your eyes to see what God is doing in your business and ministry. You may have to look two or three times before you can see it. Those who can't see are blind, and they will soon stumble over themselves, but those who tend (to look after, watch over and care for, minister to or wait on with service) will be blessed.

Prayer: Father, thank you for allowing me to see the good in spite of circumstances and situations that try to pull me off track and take my focus. Help me to fix my eyes on you so that I will not stumble and revert to my own way of doing things. When I feel discouraged, help me to look around and try to count my blessings in Jesus' name. Amen.

Day 7

Jeremiah 29:11-13, "For I know the plans I have for you," declares the Lord, "plans to prosper you and not to harm you, plans to give you hope and a future.¹² Then you will call on me and come and pray to me, and I will listen to you. ¹³ You will seek me and find me when you seek me with all your heart."

Business is a tool God has given you to win souls to the kingdom and to increase your finances. From the beginning, God was an entrepreneur. Genesis 1:1 says, **"GOD created the heavens and the earth."** The earth was formless and voided, and He worked for six days to bring the earth into a profitable state. When God created the vegetation and trees, He made sure that they were fruit-bearing so each could produce of its own kind. From that day forth, God has been reaping from residual and passive profits. He never had to plant or create the same things twice. This is exactly what God wants us to do in our business and ministries. Create. Produce. Sow. Reap.

God is using the foolish things of the world to confine the wise. God is raising people like you and me as instruments and silent weapons on the earth to carry out His will. I believe God's word that says in Isaiah 60:22, **"The least of you will become a**

thousand, and the smallest a mighty nation." Many people may have counted you out, but don't give up. God has a plan to use you to employ, create opportunities, extend favor, and open doors for others. There will be a time when your name will be made great on the earth. They may not be able to see it now, but let your light shine before men so that God may be glorified. God's glory will be revealed in you. People are going to know that God is with you. There is something different about you and about the way that you handle your business. Whether you are in business or in ministry, be a reflection of Him by operating in integrity, keeping your word, providing great customer service, offering quality products, paying above minimum wage, listening to your clients with a sincere heart, giving, and offering reasonable prices. Let people know that you can love God without wearing a Jesus t-shirt by allowing it to show in your business, ministry, and life.

Keeping God first is the key to building a sustainable and profitable business or ministry. He is the master business strategist who gives creative ideas to implement in your business and revelatory insight on how to connect with your clients to grow your business to profit, how to stand out in a saturated world, and other business tactics to prosper you. God has everything mapped out, not just in your life but in your business and ministry. You are literally put on the earth to carry out His will. He wants to use everything in your life for His purpose, and He had predestined plans for you before you were conceived in your mother's womb. Who you will become, God will disclose and communicate it to you in prayer and meditation because you were created with an identity. Whom God called you to be is more important than the bloodline you were born into. I believe that this is the reason Jesus did not have an earthly father. He wanted to show those who feel parentless that you still have His power in you to carry out His will. He gave us an example through His son, Jesus, that you don't need what others have in order to do great exploits for God. He's searching the whole earth in order to strengthen those whose hearts are fully committed to him.

What you have been assigned to do in your life and even in your business, no one else can do. You have a specific cause and mandate on your life. For this very reason, the prompting that He is giving you to do, the dreams and desires that other people can't seem to understand were all given to you by God because He has plans to use you in a specific way. Obedience is the only requirement, and when you obey God, He promises to bless you abundantly, according to Deuteronomy 28.

Prayer: Father, forgive me for not trusting you in my life and in my business. Sometimes I lose focus by thinking that everything is about me and how I want things to go in my life. Thank you for reminding me in your word that you have the plan written out for my life before I was created in my mother's womb. I was born with an objective. You know what's best for me. Teach me to seek You in all things in Jesus' name. Amen.

Day 8

Proverbs 16:3, "Commit your work to the Lord, and your plans will be established."

There should be two reasons to pursue your heart's desire: to serve others and to serve God. Many times, as leaders, we tend to think about pleasing people on our team, our clients, or our assignment in business or ministry. And we forget that God cares about everything that involves us. As Christian leaders, when you understand that God is the reason for the vision, everything should be centered around God and cultivated in prayer. God wants to be involved in all areas of your life, not just things that are spiritual. You can have the best marketing strategy, generate tons of money in your business, or have a huge following; however, success to man is not success to God. Success is when you use what you have obtained to help others. If what you're doing is only helping you pay your bills, then you're not successful. If you're only thinking about making money, then you are not in purpose. God's purpose is always tied to helping others, and success is being able to strengthen your brother and give someone an advantage. These are the opportunities that God wants to do for us through our obedience.

When you obey and trust God, He will give you the desires of your heart, of having what you define as success, and make your business sustainable and profitable. I have also seen faith-based business leaders who are super spiritual and not practical enough. Yes, prayer is imperative for wisdom and strategy; however, you have to work the vision in order to receive full rewards for your labor. You need both spiritual and practical goals.

This is why you must measure your success based upon both areas of your life and not just material gain. The devil will give you what you desire as well. The devil will always try to undermine God by attempting to give you something that God already promised you. When Jesus was in the wilderness, the devil tried to tempt Jesus by saying I will give you all of this, but Jesus was already the owner. And many things that the devil is tempting us with have already been promised to us. The devil will allow you to purchase a building when God told you to wait, just so you will struggle with keeping it and blame God for not providing or supplying for all your needs. When God blesses you, He adds no sorrow to your wealth, and usually, it takes us waiting a little longer than the quick gratification that the devil tries to fulfill.

When you spend alone time with God - in your quiet space - in your private time - your countenance should reflect the glory of God. Therefore, the light of God should be radiating in you first, then your business. This is why it is important to be committed to God, so He can establish you and His plans in your life. Don't be ruled or governed by your buyers, business objectives, revenue, or profit goals. Without God, nothing grows, matures, or progresses. You are insufficient, bankrupt, and overdrawn when you do not abide in Him. This is why many leaders become burned out on a godly assignment. Nothing supersedes having a relationship with God.

When you have done everything you know to do, and things aren't coming together or falling into place, my suggestion is to check your relationship with God. Have you been obeying God? If you trust Him, you will obey Him. One sure way to clog the flow of God is to become disobedient. Obedience allows access. Disobedience blocks access. How much time have you spent with Him? Have you been keeping your appointments with God? ***Amos 3:3 says, "How can two walk unless they have made an appointment."*** Warning: do not become too busy in your role as a leader that you forget your spiritual obligations to God. This is one of the reasons why people rise and fall and are unable to recover- they have forgotten about the One who created a way. What are you setting your affections on? Is it only making money? Is the vision clouding your judgment?

Don't allow what was meant to bless you and others to be the reason why you don't succeed. No matter where you are today, God's grace will lift you out of the pit. When Peter requested to walk upon water because he was righteous, even when His faith failed, God lifted him back up. Peter had to not only have faith in himself to get out of the boat but also in Jesus. That's why Peter had to know that Jesus wasn't going to allow Him to drown or die.

Some people rely only on their natural gifts to propel them forward, but Peter knew that he needed more than himself to do the impossible. There is no way, according to science or any other logical reason, that Peter would have had the ability to walk on water. It was only by God's power that he achieved his goal and made history. Are you trying to build your business separate from God? When you use your natural and God adds His super, you now have supernatural abilities that will allow you to make history as well.

Prayer: Father, thank you for reminding me that you are the CEO of my life, including my business. Forgive me for operating within my own strength and excluding you. I commit my actions unto you, and I will obey you in all things in Jesus' name. Amen.

Day 9

Matthew 6:33, "Seek the Kingdom of God above all else, and live righteously, and he will give you everything you need."

In a world where we are encouraged to live greedy lives, it is easy to get caught up in the world's system of imitating others, even if it means not operating in integrity by trying to rush our individual process. When we feel that God is taking too long to respond or answer what we deem urgent requests, we become tempted to fix our problems and be our own solutions. There is a way that seems right unto a man, but the end is death or destruction. If you rush the timing of God, it can delay or destroy your process.

Longsuffering is a fruit of the spirit which means that He will take us the long way, test our character and our faith, and it's part of our development to help us become more like Him. We are tested before being promoted to our next level by the way we respond to certain situations and circumstances, just like the Israelites. It wasn't God's plan to keep them in the wilderness for 40 years; however, when they were faced with a test, they did not pass. They had to stay in the process until maturity. Troubles will test your obedience to see if you are seeking God above all else, even in your lowest state of mind. When you are placed in peculiar situations, ask yourself, how would God like for me to respond or handle this situation?

As a Christian leader, we should attempt to find God's way of managing people, make Godly business decisions, and have high morals and values that pleases God. Everything that you do should be deeply rooted in love. Yes, even in your business, the way that you handle your business affairs should be grounded in the agape love of Christ. Being really concerned about matters of the heart concerning your employees and your clients will definitely take your business further. The only way that you can make God a priority as a CEO is to make Him an important factor in your everyday life. This is easier said than done when you have to manage your household, businesses, employees, spouse, and a host of other things.

Seek Him and make your time with Him a priority. As a business owner, don't be found guilty of working sun up to sun down while leaving minimal time for your family and other things that are vital to you; and especially, don't eliminate your time with God. Your purpose should always exceed profit. There may be things that you have to say no to in order to walk fully in your purpose. TD Jakes once said that when you choose purpose over profit, profit will find you. If you choose to pursue the things of this world, you will have to work harder because you haven't received guidance from the One who knows how to make every minute and hour of your day productive. God is all-knowing and when you spend time with Him, He instructs you on how to manage your life His way, but this kind of wisdom only comes when you seek Him first above all else.

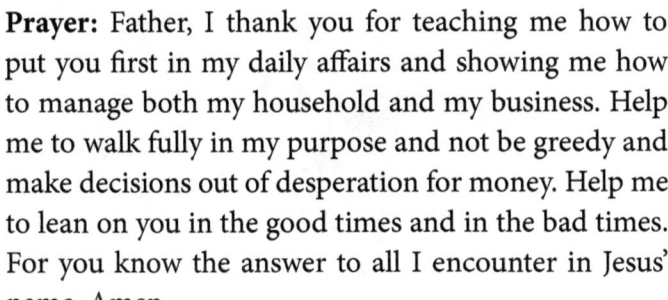

Prayer: Father, I thank you for teaching me how to put you first in my daily affairs and showing me how to manage both my household and my business. Help me to walk fully in my purpose and not be greedy and make decisions out of desperation for money. Help me to lean on you in the good times and in the bad times. For you know the answer to all I encounter in Jesus' name. Amen.

Day 10

*Philippians 4:6, "Don't worry about anything;
instead pray about everything. Tell God
what you need, and thank him for all he has done."*

Entrepreneurs have a tendency to be competitive. Sometimes the drive and hunger to be on top can cause unnecessary anxiety and worry when things don't seem to go as planned. If you are stressed, step back and take a moment to examine your situation. Where have you applied unnecessary pressure? Who is stressing you? What has attempted to take your joy? Naturally, we all want to win, but to what extent? There is an inward drive to succeed; however, don't allow your internal determination for success to cause you to be ahead of God's timeline or cause burnout.

God gave you the vision, and He will maintain it. Why panic or agonize over your business or ministry if you know God called you and you are operating within His vision? If you feel as if you are forcing things to work, you may have to make some adjustments in order for the plan to fully manifest. Write the vision down again. Revisit it. And as you are writing, you may realize that you have been operating in your own path instead of His lane.

If you become worried again, ask God to help you understand His timing and be open and transparent enough to tell Him what you need. It can be difficult to tell God what you need when you may have heard elders say not to question God and just wait on Him. However, the Lord is longing for you to be bold and courageous enough to seek Him for your company's provision. This becomes natural when you spend time in His presence and build an authentic relationship with him through prayer.

Prayer is communicating with God. You don't have to do it in a special way, just let it flow, and at the end of the dialogue, there should be a moment when you give Him time to respond and thank Him for what He has already done. The more you are appreciative of what you have accomplished, the doors that have been opened, and all He has done in your business or ministry, the more your heart will be filled with gratefulness, which rewards you with more than you can ever ask or think. If you are worried about gaining clients, finances, or growing the business, step back from it all. Clear your mind, pray, and look at what you are facing from a cup that is half full and not half empty. See your business winning, see your business on top, see your business as a household name. The more positive you become, the more you will begin to see the clutter in your mind starting to untwist and make sense. Lean not to your own understanding, but in all your ways acknowledge Him, and He will direct your path.

Prayer: Father, forgive me for worrying about my business affairs and teach me how to lean upon you when I am feeling overwhelmed and pressured. Help me to know that prayer and making my request known before you should be by first recourse instead of my last. Teach me how to rely upon you as my strength in my time of weakness in Jesus' Name, Amen.

Day 11

> *Proverbs 23:6-7, "Don't eat with people who are stingy. Don't desire their delicacies. They are always thinking about how much it costs, 'Eat and drink,' they say, but they don't mean it."*

Imagine being invited on a dinner date and you were told that you could order anything you desired without worrying about the budget, only to find out that while your date encouraged it in his or her heart, they didn't mean it. The truth is that they were doing it to impress you but really didn't have the funds to cover the cost. This is how many people operate in life, saying things to please people but not truly meaning them. God searches the heart and gives each man according to his or her motives and that's why many don't receive - because the words in their heart have more value than the words from their lips. This is one of the reasons you may not be getting the things you ask for because you're not genuinely responding to God or asking with the right intent.

Too many times, we go to God as if He doesn't already know what we are thinking or as if He doesn't know us. As a parent, there are times that I know the answer to the question that I ask my daughter. I'm checking to see her honesty and if she trusts me to be open to sharing the truth with me. God already knows. I believe breakthrough and breakout come when we go to Him unmasked. Oftentimes, we conceal our true identity from people for several reasons, including feeling unworthy to be in the presence of certain people or our past makes us feel unaccepted. Whatever the reason, we tend to go to God the same way- with a facade, then leave out of His presence, still living and being the same way we were before we went to Him. It's just like church. We will go every Sunday and leave the same. Why? Because the real us was never present. The result of this is our inability to obey, live and give as God has led us. We end up producing a life of poverty and operating from a stony heart.

Obeying God with a grudging or stingy heart is not the same, nor does it receive the same reward or response as someone who obeys with a willing and giving spirit. In addition, doing the right thing with a hardened, reluctantly, or resentful spirit will not reap the same rewards as a giving spirit.

As you climb your ladder of success, more is required of you to become a giver: a person who willingly helps and serves others with either time, talent, resources, or service as your authentic self. How far you go in life depends on how much you are willing to give. The Bible says that it is better to give than receive. The blessings are attached to your ability to give even if you feel that you don't have a lot to give. I was determined to remove poverty from my life. I came from a bloodline of hard workers, but not wealthy individuals. I saw both of my parents work extremely hard and for a long time, but both never seemed to have enough. I saw them settle and accept what life offered them, but I knew there was more. They weren't able to afford what they needed. I knew this was a life that I didn't want to live. I wanted more than anyone in my family had for the glory of God. So I started giving. I would give earrings, shoes, money, whatever I was led to give in order to break into another income bracket. And every year, our giving has increased.

My husband and I desire to be the highest contributor in our church and our community. I knew from past experiences withholding or being stingy wasn't going to break open wealth in my life. Imagine a closed fist, nothing can leave, and nothing can be received. The Bible says that He gives seed to the sower, so I knew that seed can be trusted with those who were willing to release it. The blessing about a seed is that it produces more. A seed produces after its kind, and a well-watered, cultivated seed turns into a harvest. A harvest can be given away, sold for revenue, invested, and replanted as a seed so it will always meet a need and supply for you. Therefore I opened my hand and decreed that as easily as it came in, as easily I was going to release it by the leading of the Holy Spirit.

Your position as a leader gives you the responsibility to assist others to become better. And you don't have to wait until your business generates a certain amount of money in order to support and break stinginess from your life.

> *John 12:24 says, "Unless a seed is planted in the soil and dies, it remains alone. But its death will produce many new kernels - a plentiful harvest of new lives."*

When you do something for people, and you really don't mean it - or you keep reminding yourself of what you have done for that person, the seed you have planted is not dead. It is still alive, therefore, you are not receiving the harvest from it. Harvest only comes when you give from the sincerity of your heart, forget about it, and allow it to come back to you in other ways.

Prayer: Father, help me to be a cheerful giver so that I can be positioned to help others and be trusted with more. Forgive me when I trusted more in what's in my hand than what was in your hand for my life. Today I commit to giving more financially and with my life in Jesus' name. Amen.

Day 12

> *2 Timothy 1:7, "For God has not given us a spirit of fear and timidity, but of power, love, and self-discipline."*

Fear is the stumbling block that keeps many leaders from succeeding in business because it requires you to do something that you may not have seen done before, or maybe you're the first one to take a leap of faith in your family. Whatever the reason is for allowing fear to be the driving force in your life, it will consume your hopes and your dreams. You will never become all that God has for you when you allow fear to have a place in your life.

It is important to understand there are two kinds of fear: the emotion of fear and the spirit of fear. The biggest difference between the two types of fear is that you can be emotionally fearful and still do the will of God. The spirit of fear will paralyze you and keep you from being able to move forward. It literally stops you every time you even think about moving forward. This is the one that many people wrestle with the most.

The spirit of fear will cause you to live an empty, unfilled life. Think about your business or ministry; what would you really do if fear wasn't present? How would your life be different if fear wasn't ruling your decisions? Fear is a silent vision killer. It speaks to your areas of insecurity. It stands against your identity and makes you feel as if you don't have what it takes to be you. Let's be clear; you are prepackaged with all the tools and abilities you need in order to succeed in life and in your business. You were created with them.

You may feel that what you have been called to do is bigger than what's inside of you. And that is true. The reason that it is larger than you is so that you can rely on GOD to help you do what seems impossible. Your dream was never meant to be accomplished by you alone or to fit within your small space. You may feel uneducated, inexperienced, or like you just don't know how to manifest the vision. First, you must avoid allowing fear to steal your confidence. In Exodus, the Lord instructed Moses to lead the people out of Egypt, but his first excuse was his deficiency - his inability to speak well. But God still chose Him. You're called, anointed, and appointed for such a time as this and even if you feel underqualified, God still predestined you before you were shaped in your mother's womb, in spite of how you see yourself. It is what God has placed inside of you that makes you more than adequate.

One of the most important strategies to overcoming fear and relying on the power that's inside of you is prayer. Communicating with God is the only ammunition that destroys the yokes of the evil one. During prayer, you are refueled, recharged, and realigned with God's purpose for your life. Without a consistent prayer life, you will always feel incapable and overwhelmed with getting to your next level, which, I believe, is one of the reasons that businesses fail. Relying on your own strength limits your growth in you, in your company, and in your teammates. Their development depends on you receiving wisdom, knowledge, understanding, and downloads from God to help you overcome fear; then you're positioned to help them overcome their obstacles and fear. The people whom you are called to lead depend on you to push them in faith and overcome fear.

If you don't conquer fear, you will subconsciously lead people right into fear. How you feel, they will feel. Everything that I have tried to hide from my daughter, I see operating in her because she watches what I do and listens to everything that I say, more than I know. When fear shows up in your current state, make a choice to push through by making a conscious decision to stay focused on your goals and respond to it with your faith. Do the opposite of what fear wants you to do. If fear says quit, then by faith keep going. This time, respond differently to fear. You may want to ask yourself questions to see where the fear is coming from, especially if you find it showing up when it is time for you to make decisions. What is causing the war inside of you? Are you afraid of failure? Are you afraid of what people may say about you? What is causing your battle?

Once you pinpoint the root of your fear, which may be showing up in other areas of your life as well, then create a plan. The only reason fear sets in (brews, remains, stays around, manifests) is that there is no plan and no execution. Fear operates in the unknown. Next time you are feeling fearful, try speaking with someone who will give you Godly counsel to help ease your anxiety. Sometimes all you need is wise counsel to help you see past your fear. You'll be surprised how talking with others who have traveled a similar path will calm your fears.

Prayer: Father, help me to defeat fear by stepping out in faith. For you have not given me the spirit of fear but of power, love, and a sound mind. I decree clarity in my mind, vision, business, and soul. In Jesus' name, Amen!

Day 13

Deuteronomy 8:18, "Remember the Lord your God. He is the one who gives you power to be successful, in order to fulfill the covenant he confirmed to your ancestors with an oath."

On your journey, people will applaud you and pat you on the back for your amazing and many accomplishments. They will make your head big and sit you on the mountaintop; however, you must remember the Lord, your God, and not become pompous in your success. People will make it easy for you to feel as if it is your own abilities that are causing success around you. However, the power that is working inside of you - your potential - has been given by God as a testament of His abilities to manifest Himself in the natural world, through your willingness. So once they start making you big, make Him even bigger. This will keep you humble and your heart right before God. Acknowledging the One who is greater than you will keep you low and humble in spirit.

Saul was upset and stepped outside the will of God because the people were saying that he had only killed thousands and that David killed ten thousand. He listened to what the people were saying, and it pushed him outside the will of God, and he eventually lost his dominion. Saul had forgotten that it was God who was giving him the victory.

Without God, there is no success. Many individuals start out in Him, and it seems to be easier to do if you come from an impoverished background. People tend to be more thankful and grateful that they have made it through the storm. Take Tyler Perry, a multi-billionaire who came from homelessness who shares His faith through his sitcoms, plays, and other productions. Then there are others that forget God, and they stop everything they were doing to get to where they are. They stop praying, going to church, serving, and just about everything spiritual. The enemy will make them feel as if they don't have the time, or they will get a big head and feel as if they are too successful to be doing certain things. A clear definition of pompous. The higher you climb, the more cognizant you must become to include God.

You need God to make wise decisions, to lead, and to be successful. That's why having a dedicated time of prayer helps you maneuver as a leader and helps you discover ways to implement biblical principles in your business.

Consider Chick-Fil-A, for instance… they could be open on Sundays; however, they have adopted, as part of their business model, not to work on Sundays in order to give employees opportunities to rest, spend time with friends and families, and to attend worship if they choose. Therefore, God allows the business to prosper without compromising what's important to them. Don't climb and lose sight of God. You can be successful, have integrity in your endeavors and still honor God. As you go higher, you may have to pull away from others and say no to certain business deals to keep your core values, and when you do, you will have more success than you could have ever imagined.

God will give you spiritual wisdom and understanding to face and overcome every circumstance that arises in your business or ministry. Situations and circumstances will happen that are out of your control, but when God is in the midst, He will empower you and guide you. He's your instructor, and every good teacher wants to see their students succeed.

Whatever area you may be struggling in today, pray over it; invite God in and watch the outcome. You will come out on top. You will win. Victory belongs to you. Choose His way and never forget Him along the way.

Prayer: Father, help me to stay focused on you and not to allow my foundation to crumble when making business decisions. Help my faith to shine so that you may be glorified when I'm faced with various trials and tribulations in my life. May your words be hidden in my heart that I may not sin against it. I invite you in to help me and guide me into all truth so that we can be successful in Jesus' name. Amen.

Day 14

Titus 3:14 - "Our people have to learn to be diligent in their work so that all necessities are met (especially among the needy) and they don't end up with nothing to show for their lives." (MSG version)

Measure the development of your team by the way they respond to people, circumstances, and situations based upon your leadership. Your business or ministry is built upon your shoulders. You are the example, and those whom you lead are watching carefully. Therefore, it is important to exhibit love, even when you have to chastise and discipline others. If you treat others well, God will treat you well. And your team will duplicate your faith.

You can only expect from your team what you are willing to give. If you have a strong work ethic, then it's easier to expect others on your team to have a strong work ethic as well. When you set the bar, your tolerance level will not allow you to expect less than what you give.

Your level of commitment and performance is the gauge used to evaluate those under your leadership. It is your duty to ensure that people who are assigned to projects and those who work at any capacity in your business are hard workers, and their value is a reflection of yours. What you value and your morals will be shown by the way you influence others and how they implement it in your business. Your team is appointed to represent you in their responsibilities, and you are appointed to be a portrait of the Father. Therefore, you can not allow bad habits, attitudes, tardiness, or laziness to go unaddressed in your business, even if they are a top performer. Choose character over abilities. You can teach a person to have a skill set, but you can not train a person to have values. **Proverbs states that a good name is to be chosen over great riches.**

Hold individuals accountable for their actions; otherwise, you are endorsing conduct that does not align with your vision. Being a CEO is more than just saying that you own a company; you also become an advisor. People are connected to you for more than a job. You become their teacher and role model. Even if they don't work for you for a long period of time, you should influence them to become better than they were before they came to your company.

God will use your business or ministry as a tool to help others in a way that only you can, such as s giving someone a chance who may have never had an opportunity to work for a company like yours. Make a difference and show appreciation at all times. Instead of firing them, train them. Instead of demoting them, find a position that really showcases their skills. People tend to work harder and are more dedicated to the vision when they see that you care more about them than their ability to make you money. Pray for your team. Ask God to reveal the purpose and position He has in mind for them and work towards fulfilling God's will in their life through your business.

Remember, people who work in your business do not just work for you; they are essentially working for your Heavenly Father. When people work for your company, they become your assignment, and you must train them to become either good leaders or good managers. Build with people who understand the vision and figure out a way to make them feel valuable. Once a person believes in the vision and knows you care, they become vested. As you excel, they should as well. I declare that you are building a winning team.

Prayer: Father, I thank you for teaching me how to be a great leader and for helping me to lead in such a way that you may be glorified. Help me to be the demonstration of your love, your forgiveness, and your compassion for others, even in my business. Let your word take root in my heart so that it is easily reflected even if I am upset. Help me to remember you and to lean on you when I feel that I am overwhelmed or stressed out in Jesus' name. Amen.

Day 15

> *Isaiah 45:3, NIV "I will give you hidden treasures, riches stored in secret places, so that you may know that I am the Lord, the God of Israel, who summons you by name."*

As a CEO, many times you will feel alone and as if others don't understand your logic, thinking, or risk you are willing to take in business, and more than likely, they won't. People will not fully understand what God has given you or the reason why you are willing to sacrifice the way that you do. God has given you the inside scoop. The innovative ideas, creative thoughts, and the things that come easy for you are concealed from others and revealed to you. He said that He will give you hidden treasures. He will give you witty ideas and strategies to break open wealth in your life. When times are tough in business, it may feel as if God doesn't care about your profit and loss statement or your marketing strategy. In fact, He cares about everything that concerns you, but have you been obedient in your business? Did you post when He told you to? Do you show up consistently? Is your faith in action? Did you share your services when He led you to? Obedience is the key to having access to hidden treasures. If He wanted everyone to know or to have the key, He wouldn't have hidden it.

God will give you multi-million dollar business ideas, give you favor with people in high places, and take a little and multiply it by thousands. People will drive past similar businesses just to spend money with you. He will give you the edge over all your competitors. People will send for you from other countries, celebrities will request to work with you, and you will have access to everything you need in order to be successful if you obey. God is on your side. He wants you to win, and He will reveal more and more to you that won't be detected with the naked eye.

While you are going through the process and trying to figure everything out, don't be afraid to take a chance on God. Very similar to the scripture that says if you bring your tithe and offering in the storehouse, you can test Him in this, and He will open the windows of heaven for you, such that you will not have enough room to receive. With every testing and act of obedience, treasures will be released unto you. Test God, He won't fail you. Step out on His word, and He won't let you down. When things don't align immediately, don't panic. Continue to trust and stand on His word. Right now, you may feel tested. Don't fret. The real owner of your company wants to know if you will stand with Him through the storm and the rain. He will reveal Himself to you, and you will know that He is GOD: the One who is with you.

There is a passage in the Bible where Hagar was running away from her mistress Sarai, who was antagonizing her after she had only obeyed her request to sleep with Abraham. Now she was in an emotional state that caused her to run away, but the angel of the Lord said go back. Don't run. Submit to her authority. I have seen your pain Hagar, and I will give you a son. Hagar had to be willing to go back to the place of hurt and submit to the very one that caused her so much grief. She had to face her fear, but God saw her. He saw her pain. And the Bible says that she named that place, Beer-lahai-roi, which means well of the Living One

Who Sees Me. God saw her and rewarded her. You may be tested beyond what you think you can endure, but God sees you, and you will know that He is with you.

Starting your business or ministry is not by mistake. It may feel like it at times. You may be asking yourself, "why in the world did I start this business?" You're losing sleep, money, time, and maybe even hair, but it's by divine manifestation and revelation. It's the Lord's will, and He will bless you for it. God is willing and ready to give you the riches stored in secret places, but you have to be willing to do what others aren't in order to get what they won't have. It's similar to trying to find a needle in a haystack. Some people will not look at all to find it. It's too much trouble; others will look for a short period of time, then there will be individuals who won't stop looking until they find it. Perseverance will cause you to discover things that others won't find. They gave up too quickly. They thought it would be easier and better to buy another one. You will always learn something that you didn't know when you seek what can't be seen. Will you be the one that perseveres and endures until the end? Will you stay until your reward comes? The treasures are available for everyone, but only a few are able to receive them. He gave His Son to the entire world, so whosoever believes in Him will not perish but have everlasting life. It's available to the whosoevers.

Stay in it and if God calls you to it, He will bring you through it and reward you greatly.

Prayer: Father, I thank you for revealing your secrets to me and giving me access to hidden and unknown things that can't be seen with the natural eye. Help me to remain consistent and keep you in my foresight. I refuse to quit. I refuse to give up in Jesus' name. Amen.

Day 16

> *Joshua 1:8, "This book of the law shall not depart from your mouth, but you shall meditate on it day and night, so that you may be careful to do according to all that is written in it; for then you will make your way prosperous, and then you will have success."*

When building a family, business, house, or establishing anything, the infrastructure is the most important element of the structure. If the foundation is weak, anything erected upon it becomes fragile and will not last. Therefore, if you try to build your business on anything other than the Word of God, it will not stand. According to research, 8 out of 10 businesses will fail, so can you imagine how much that percentage will increase when you don't have biblical principles implemented in your business? You'll experience greater levels of what might have naturally occurred but to a higher degree. This is one of the reasons that individuals make it to a certain point and then they fall off. They allowed the Word to depart from their mouth. If the Word isn't in your mouth, then it's not in your heart, and it won't be found in your life.

The scripture is charging you to use the growth and success of your business as a measuring tool to gauge whether or not you have obeyed Him in your life. Your business or ministry will be a reflection of your personal walk with Him. If you struggle with allowing God to be a part of your regular life, you will struggle with allowing Him into your business or ministry. You'll only be duplicating habits; therefore, you will get the same results. For instance, if you are a poor manager of finances in your household, then you will more than likely become a poor manager in your business. Sometimes we feel that we will do things better or differently if we have another outlet. The truth is those same bad habits or principles will eventually show up in other areas of your life. The only way to counterattack this response is to change your entire life, not just parts of it. You can't change your business and leave your life the same. You have to change your life, so your business will reap. If you try to change your business only, then your regular life will remain the same. I hope this makes sense. So in essence, you can't run from change if you want to build a sustainable life which includes your business or ministry. You're not separate from them; you are them. This is why you have to engage in thought the word of God. Only then will you be able to make changes that will last and positively reflect your life. Are you considering or consulting Him when you make a decision or when you need direction? Are you thinking about His word as you make your day-to-day decisions?

Oftentimes, people have a hard time really understanding what it means to live more like Him or to include Him. It doesn't mean that you are quoting every scripture. Remember, the devil quoted scriptures too, yet he was the same one who thought he was like God. It's being able to apply it and live it. Being in business or ministry does not exclude you from operating in the principles of God. As a matter of fact, as a Christian leader, you should display more of God, for example, how quickly you forgive, how you treat your team, and how you respect and honor those who may be lower in status than you. As a matter of fact, you are held even more accountable since you are the teacher and shepherd who is responsible for winning and leading those in your business or ministry. Your pulpit and the ministry of Jesus Christ are displayed in your day-to-day interactions with people. Use your business as a ministry tool and as an opportunity to display His Word.

In the startup phase of business or ministry, it seems to be easier for people to trust God because they have no other choice. Their faith in motion. But when you have notoriety and start generating profit in your business, will you abandon the tools, resources, and sources that have allowed you to be successful? As a contingency, if you obey what is written, He will make your ways prosperous, then you will have success.

> **Prayer:** Father, forgive me for anytime that I have allowed your word to depart from my mouth. May I never forget your word and the benefits and blessings attached to obeying your word. Help me to walk in obedience with you in my business and ministry, with my team and clients, so that you can make my ways prosperous in Jesus' name. Amen.

Day 17

Isaiah 48:10- "Behold, I have refined you, but not as silver, I have tested you in the furnace of affliction."

As a CEO, you will notice that individuals who are a part of your team are talented in many areas. And the gifts that have been given to each person should be used to serve others. The gift is pure, but the person may be contaminated. Therefore, teammates should be tested and tried like gold that is purified. They may be the perfect fit for your company, or they may be able to fill a gap or a role that has been vacant, yet they still need to go through the process before you release the reins for them to operate solely in that position. If their motives are genuine, it will be proven. But with all things, tests are important to determine whether or not a person is ready for the next level. It is a very similar process that God takes you through in life, and without being able to pass the test, you can't elevate to the next level. This is the reason that people can't take your success away because you've earned the right to be where you are today. You've passed many tests through the afflictions that come with building a business or ministry. Actually, the afflictions that you have been through it should prove your character. Character is proven not with words but through actions during tough times. Everybody can make the right decisions when things are going well or when they have what they need. But the moment that trials come, they are pushed beyond what they think they can handle; that's when you pay close attention to their response to pressure.

Many people didn't make it. Some quit in the middle of their process and never get a chance to see what the end results were going to be. They miss their reward. When crummy things happen to you or in your business, God's not mistreating you. He is getting you ready. It is during those hard and challenging times that God is freeing you from impurities by getting you prepared for the next level of success. With every refinement, there is a reward.

Process comes before promotion. Your responsibility as a leader is to put a process in place to assist with developing people and their gifts, before promotion. That's why many jobs have evaluation periods to watch the performance of the individuals.

What I have discovered through the years is that you can teach a skill set, but there are certain characteristics either they have, or they don't. This is why I choose character over gifts and conditions. In addition, when there is an unfilled position in your company, it is easy to concentrate on one's ability, then later discover what you really needed was trustworthy, honest, and loyal people. In order for your business to grow, you must have the right people on your team and in the right position. If a person shows they are untrustworthy, then trust that is the real them at this moment. Can they change? Absolutely they can; however, you must use discernment as to where to place them in your business.

Being a Christian doesn't mean you should ignore the warning signs known as the spirit of discernment. The Lord knows everything about a person, even the parts of us that we try to hide; therefore, you may not be able to place your finger on what you are discerning, but you can trust Him to reveal it to you in time; especially when a person is rebuked or disciplined.

Hurt reveals all things. When a person is offended or they don't get their way, that is the time that you should be most mindful and watchful. Wounded emotions or a hurt heart always reveal the motives and intentions of a person. That's why the Lord tests us in the furnace of afflictions. He knows how you will respond; He just wants you to see you. Oftentimes, we can't see ourselves until we see ourselves through the fire of affiliation.

Prayer: Father, give me strength to pass every test and to know that you are only processing me to prepare me for the next phase of my life and business. Help me not to take what is happening as offense or punishment from you, but as your genuine love and concern for me in Jesus' name, Amen.

Day 18

Ecclesiastes 11:2 - "Invest in seven ventures, yes, in eight; you do not know what disaster may come upon the land."

The worst thing that you can do is have all your eggs in one basket. What happens when all your eggs break? The way the economy is today, it is not as easy as it has been in the past to obtain a job that pays you equivalent to what you are worth or what you can generate in your business. In 2008, when we started ministry, it was the same year that I was laid off from my job. Thankfully, I had other revenue streams. As a CEO, you are not limited to producing one stream of income.

In church or as a Christian, we are taught that desiring to have more in life is a sign of greed. And that can be the truth if you are driven by money. But God is showing you that it is important to diversify our income and not have it in one place. I believe that it is sin not to go after everything that God has given you and what He wants for you.

As a kingdom-driven entrepreneur, the wealth you obtain should be to fulfill the needs of you and others. ***In Acts 2:44, "It says that the believers met together in one place and shared everything they had. They sold their property and possessions and shared***

the money with those in need." As a matter of fact, when you start pursuing your purpose, you will find that you are multi-talented and gifted to produce wealth for yourself and others. The more wealth you obtain, the more you should challenge yourself to give. Therefore, you should be tapping into all your resources and skill sets in order to develop new and many streams of income in order to become a contributor to society and donate to many good causes.

Your wealth does not have to come out of one category. Perhaps, if you are good at administration, you may have an opportunity to invest in an accounting business or a network marketing business. Don't close the doors to opportunities because you are used to operating in one arena. There are various ways to make money. Stretch the vision and evaluate where you have been closing off your heart to other streams of income. There are many ways to make your money work for you: investing in other companies, starting a new company, writing a book, renovating houses, and franchising, are just a few.

Don't allow comfort or the fear of failure to keep you from going to the next level. It is time that you start seeking other ways to generate income in your business and ministry.

As a business owner, you should have both products and services that you are offering to your client. As a rule of thumb, bring your business to profit and make sure it is sustainable before you venture into a new business. Grow where you are, then take the skills, resources, and tools that you gained in your current position to propel you quicker in your next venture. Once you learn the art of building a business, duplicate it as many times as your abilities will allow you. We see it all the time: you can dominate in ministry and the marketplace. You can have both. You don't have to choose just ministry. You can operate in ministry and still dominate in entrepreneurship.

Prayer: Father, thank you for showing me in your word that I can have many streams of income. Help me to open up my ears to new opportunities and new ways of earning additional money to use for great causes in Jesus' name. Amen.

Day 19

Proverbs 11:14- "Where there is no counsel, the people fall, but in the multitude of counselors there is safety."

In order to grow your business, you must be able to delegate and train others to operate effectively in their role. Since you are the visionary for the company, everything can not be delegated. It is the anointing of your life that becomes the lifeline of the company; therefore, everything must start and end with you. Without your guidance and direction, the business will fail. Like Jesus, He discipled twelve individuals, and He kept three of the disciples very close to Him. If you were to adopt this same method in your business, identify a leader for every department, then adopt a core team who can handle your responsibilities when you are unavailable. Now you have positioned yourself as the CEO or Overseer of the company. How many times do you really see CEOs working in the business? Rarely. Their time is more suited to oversee and create and develop the business for growth. Therefore, your communication is mainly with the leaders and the core team. If you are a one-person team, you will more than likely become the brand behind your company, so you will need help with fulfilling requests, or something will be lacking. However, you decide to manage your company, remember that instructions must come from you until your team or your leaders show, through conversation and actions, that they can perform effectively without your immediate supervision.

Keep in mind it is important to keep your paws on each and every leader and know what is going on in your company. You shouldn't ever be blind-sided. There are people who will be more talented and gifted than you, but this is your company. Be open to changes and suggestions, but you must remain present in your business or ministry.

In one of our businesses, we had become very comfortable with a person on our leadership team. We were not as hands-on in that office as we should have been, and we paid a hefty cost for it. The next year, the leader left and took the entire team. Yes, we were hurt and heartbroken, but the truth is that we set ourselves up for that loss, and we take full responsibility for it because there was no counsel. We relied on the guidance of the one we put in charge, and God had to show us that we had mismanaged her and our responsibility as a leader - we never gave counsel or correction. Keep your hands and eyes on your business and address what seems unusual. Every leader needs a leader or an accountability person, including you.

> **Prayer:** Father, help me to understand that you have placed the vision inside of me, and it is important to guide my team to win. They need the instructions that you have placed inside of me. Even when I feel incompetent, send the right people who can assist me when I feel weak. As you take me to the top, help me to rely and trust the right people that can provide me safety. In Jesus' name. Amen

Day 20

1 Peter 2:2- "Like newborn babies, crave pure spiritual milk, so that by it you may grow up in your salvation."

You are constantly at war choosing between good and evil, thus, the Bible becomes the instrument to help you choose the right course of action and make decisions that please Him even in your business. You will always have to make a choice. Everything in life is about a decision, and you are one decision away from the top or bottom. Decisions are monitored by the way you treat your team, whether you are paying them fairly or the way you usurp your authority. His eyes are in every place, beholding the good and the evil. Therefore, our mode of operation should be based upon the Word of God, which requires you to obey Him; and your obedience to Him will cause you to treat people fairly. The more you follow His statutes and allow Him to be in charge, the more you become like Him and a target for both God and your adversary.

The enemy doesn't play fair with believers. The attacks are intensified the higher you rise, because the enemy is after those who surrender to the will of the Father. But God is also after those who surrender to His will, and when you do right by God, He will lift up a standard against the enemy. He will draw the line in the sand, and the devil will only be able to go so far, like with Job. When the devil wanted to test Job, God gave him permission to do so and put stipulations in place. He told the devil you can test him, but you cannot kill him. The Lord was drawing the line and restricted his actions.

In order to be led by the Spirit, there is another degree that you must rise to in your thinking that reflects in your business or ministry. In order to do so, you must crave more of God. Your business will not exceed your spiritual growth. Everything is based upon the Word of God. He is the foundation. Therefore, you must seek Him with a sincere heart in order to level up, so you must desire strongly to be more like Him. Oftentimes people crave success; however, their focus and purpose should be to desire the sincere milk of the Word so they may grow.

God is the same today, yesterday, and forever more, but you shouldn't be. You have to grow in the Word and live by it. Growth isn't measured by your material standards because God will give you the things that you desire such as a nice house, car, but it must not be coveted above your ambition to be like Him. Evaluate where you are today versus where you were six months to a year ago. Challenge yourself to grow as a leader. In what areas do you want to g; thus a believer and leader?

Prayer: Father, forgive me when I have desired a successful business more than I was driven to get to know You and learn more of your Word. Help me to realize that all things are possible to those who believe, and those who seek your face will grow both naturally and spiritually in Jesus' name. Amen.

Day 21

Hebrews 13: 7 - "Remember your leaders, who spoke the word of God to you. Consider the outcome of their way of life and imitate their faith."

As a CEO, you are the standard in your business or ministry, and those you lead will follow your example. Your team is a great template of your leadership, and they will copy the habits of the people who are closest to them, you and the other teammates. For this reason, it is important to hire the right people and build great leaders in your circle. If you're a parent, you begin to see the things that you find amusing in your child or the things that you don't like based upon what your child does. Initially, you may question where they learned certain behaviors, words, or patterns; then you may quickly realize they absorb faster the very thing that you do versus what you say or habits and traits that you think they didn't notice. This is an example of how individuals develop around you. They imitate what you do before they listen to what you say. As human beings, we are created to lead and follow.

Every leader needs a leader: someone they can turn to discuss ideas, shifts, growths, failures or just have someone to lean on. The Bible mentions having wise counseling because what sounds good to you may not be necessarily good for you right now. Doing the right thing at the wrong time is still wrong. Start praying that God will send leaders to your company and that you will be a good steward over the individuals that you are called to lead.

You have probably heard the saying, "birds of a feather flock together." You can start to identify your team based upon groups or the individuals they hang around the most in your company. Behavior influences behavior. Iron sharpens iron. People influence people. Leaders will always be drawn to other leaders. What are you showing your leadership team? Colleagues? Clients? Are you negative? Do you complain all the time? Do you see the worst before you see the best? Remember, they will imitate your faith and actions or the lack thereof.

Prayer: Father, help me to realize that I sharpen those who are around me. Help me to realize that I should be careful not to lead people the wrong way with my actions, words, or faith. Help me to stand strong in my faith and I should be a great representative of you at all times in Jesus' name. Amen.

Day 22

> *Proverbs 13:11 ESV - "Wealth gained hastily will dwindle, but whoever gathers little by little will increase it."*

Can you imagine graduating from kindergarten and immediately being promoted to a senior in college? This is a prime example of what individuals crave when they start out in business. Initially, it does sound good to skip the line and progress ahead of the ones you started with, but are you prepared to handle the mental and emotional state of a college student with an elementary mentality? Absolutely not! That's how quickly most people want success - straight to the top.

In today's society, most individuals desire to have money, fame, fortune, and a successful business almost immediately. However, it's the journey that teaches us the true meaning of success. You will be taught lifelong lessons that will help you to prosper God's way when you learn to embrace the ride and understand how even your failures will become the tour to triumph. The roads you have to travel in life - and there will be many - will teach you things that you will never forget, and they will help you to grow as a business leader. As a matter of fact, they will help you make better choices and create a lifestyle that is pleasing to God.

True success is birthed over time. God gave Joseph a dream that he was going to have great success. Joseph was so excited about it that he began to share it with his family, but God couldn't avoid taking him through the process which was necessary for the development of him as a person who would eventually lead a nation. The timeline for your success will be different. It may be longer, or it may be shorter than others, but don't try to skip the process. Have you heard the saying that anything worth having is worth waiting for? This is true when it comes to promotion and increase that truly comes from God. Valuable goods take longer to produce. It may not take everyone the same amount of time, but real gold has to be tested and purified. There will be a season in your business or ministry where you are planting many seeds, but if you watch over them and cultivate the seeds like farmers, you can expect your harvest to come.

As a leader, it is easy to deceive, lie or misuse others to climb to the top. Think about genetically modified fruit. Do you think it is as good for your body as organically grown fruit? Whatever is gained quickly outside of God doesn't last long and does not have the ability to reproduce. That's why some people jump into pyramid schemes - looking for quick money. They want it artificially. However, the greatest lessons in life are birthed through the storm, pain, letdowns, and misfortune.

It may appear that others are climbing quicker and higher and running faster than you, but you don't know their story. As a CEO, don't compare. Stay in your lane and run the race that has been created for you. You don't know how they got there. Why are you looking? You should be so focused on your business or ministry that you don't have time to count the blessings of others. Keep your eyes focused on your assignment and on Christ. Your time is coming. Be patient. Be consistent. Be innovative. Be creative. Be obedient. And as Paul said, he learned to be content with a little or a lot.

Impatience leads to unnecessary mistakes and choices that will delay the timing of God. Don't interfere with God's plan by trying to obtain wealth hastily. Be willing to be last. For those who are last shall be first. Little by little. One step at a time. Increase shall come.

Prayer: Father, teach me to wait patiently on you and not to get impatient in my seed of sowing and planting. Help me to show up, hard work, be consistent, and a good steward over what you have given me now. For in due season, I will reap a harvest if I faint not in Jesus' name, Amen.

Day 23

Proverbs 21:5. "Good planning and hard work lead to prosperity, but hasty shortcuts lead to poverty."

Being a CEO can be draining, tiresome, and require more hours than you ever intended to put into your business; however, it will all pay off. You may be tempted to step outside of God's will in your business by taking shortcuts and following your own way. Initially, it may seem easier and quicker to deviate from God's plan, but it can lead to a dangerous outcome. Be willing to work harder than anybody in your company and stand boldly on God's word to trust the vision that He has given you.

All it takes is one wrong decision to take you further than you intended and longer to get back on course. Don't get caught up in the heat of the moment. There's never a safe route when you pursue anything outside of God's will. Your security and safety should be in Him. If you plan it, write it down, take it to God to receive His stamp of approval, and stay in His will. God doesn't bless what He doesn't approve, nor does He authorize doors to open or give favor to anything that He isn't in. Therefore if you make your own bed, you better be willing to lie in it.

Oftentimes, we make our own way without understanding that our business is not our own. This is a joint venture. It belongs to God, and He is your accountability partner and should be consulted before making decisions. He watches over everything that you do and say, and he rewards you with success according to what you deserve.

You are God's plan. You are a little god on the earth; created in His likeness. You are not a mistake. You were created on purpose. You are approved. God cares about the things that concern you, so when you become discouraged, ask God to strengthen you. CEOs tend to make permanent decisions based upon their temporary circumstances. At the time, the situation may seem as if it is unchangeable, but you should be the one that has unmovable and unshakable faith. Don't allow what you are going through to change your belief. Rely on Him. Let Him be your way of escape. You can work hard, smart, make a lot of money, and be in His will. As my pastor, Bishop Jonathan Woods, Sr. says, "YOU CAN BE RIGHTEOUS & RICH.

The most successful people in life aren't those who are given a silver spoon but those who had to go through the struggle and were determined to come out. They gained and earned success over time. No shortcuts.

Prayer: Father, help me to plan for success in my business or ministry by writing down the vision, working hard, and being mindful of your instructions. Open up my eyes to see the strategy that you have for my lifelong success that you have for me. I confess today that I am willing to take the long route as long as I'm in your will. In Jesus' name. Amen.

Day 24

> *Exodus 23:12 NIV - "Six days do your work,*
> *but on the seventh day do not work, so that your ox*
> *and your donkey may rest, and so that the slave born*
> *in your household and the foreigner living among you*
> *may be refreshed."*

If you are feeling overwhelmed, frustrated, short-tempered, or exhausted, these are all signs of stress and a lack of rest. You have to practice relaxing your mind, emotions, spirit, and natural body to properly be able to think clearly and to be able to fully execute God's plans for your business or ministry. Moments when you feel irritable for unknown reasons or drained or when everything seems to be an emergency or urgent and the to-do list never seems to come to an end; it's time to reset your life.

Oftentimes leaders struggle with turning off their brain, phone, and social media to focus on them. Your business will only grow as you grow. When you are anxious, you will subconsciously make those around you feel rushed. Therefore, you should schedule time to refresh your mind and spirit. When was the last time that you took time to meditate, pray, and sleep without distractions? Put it on your calendar once a month, to take time just for you to be refilled by God and receive the fresh faith and power that you need in order to continue to empower your team and stay on top of your game. What can you rearrange or delegate to others from your business? What can you simply cut off? What are you missing in your business that is keeping you from getting the adequate rest you need?

Entrepreneurship is about being able to do the things that you love, including the freedom to create your own schedule. Don't allow your business to run you. You must learn to stay in control of your business, time, and money, or it will all consume you. If your office hours are 9-5, then don't feel as if you will miss money if you don't respond to an e-mail or fulfill a customer request after hours. Those things should be done if you want to after hours, but not out of obligation. You need your off time to properly refresh your mind, body, and soul. Otherwise, you will find yourself giving off negative energy and vibes.

You are built like a car: it can only move when you put gas in it, and without proper maintenance, even a full tank of gas isn't enough to keep it going. However, you can increase the usefulness of it when it has been properly maintained. Your business can function without you for at least half of a day to spend time in prayer with God and resting in His presence.

Remember that He is the boss, and you follow His lead by getting the mental and emotional break that you need to be an effective and efficient CEO. Your business will not grow to the level of success you desire with cluttered thoughts.

You'll be unable to be creative if you don't take the time to refresh your mind. Rest is just as important as money!

Prayer: Father, help me to not feel pressured by money to work outside my allotted time for business or ministry. I will not lose the things and people who are important to me. Help me to manage all that you have given me wisely. I declare that I am a good steward over my family, finances, friends, and business in Jesus' name. Amen.

Day 25

Psalm 142:3, NLT "When I am overwhelmed, you alone know the way I should turn."

Being a leader is very challenging. It is one of the most difficult responsibilities that you may have endured, along with being a spouse, a parent, and a list of other roles that you have had to accept. You may find it hard to balance everything that comes with being you, especially if you are the strong one in your family or you bounce back more quickly than others.

With the drive and tenacity that you have, oftentimes, in your weakest moments, you are overlooked. You may feel isolated. Alone. Abandoned. Simply because others don't see or understand the weight that you have to carry. This is normal. People only see your outside persona and how resilient you are. Many people depend on you to be their strength. Others perceive you to be almost perfect, as if you have it all together, but the reality is that you may be frustrated and tired more than people can perceive. So this is how you have learned to cope with life - pretending that you have it all together - or ignoring your true feelings. The truth is, sometimes you're worn out, and you need someone to be a shoulder for you. There is a part of you that might have wanted to scream, run your car off the side of the road, or pack up and leave everything that you have worked so hard to accomplish. Again, this is normal.

And it is okay. It is natural to feel this way. Every successful person goes through it. I have been there. Although you may have a consistent prayer life, go to church, and try to live right, these are still your true emotions. You aren't perfect. The beauty of being a believer is that the Holy Spirit won't allow you to walk away from your leadership role because He is upholding you in His hand. But He will give you space to feel your emotions and take care of you. When Elijah was battling depression, the Lord fed him; took care of him.

When you are weak, His power is being made strong in your life. You may be emotionally drained, spiritually tired, and mentally tapped out, but God won't let you go. He won't allow you to give up. He will be your strength when you feel that you can't take anymore, and He will be your solution if you express your truth to Him. Ask God for what you need and be open to receiving His direction and guidance. He will answer you in various ways by allowing you to read an inspirational post on social media or when you are listening to a song on the radio, through conversation, prayer, or meditation. He wants to help you. If you seek Him, you will find Him. You aren't alone.

God wants to show up for you, and He will walk with you through the valleys and on the mountaintop. He's faithful. And His timing is perfect. You don't have to hold it together, He does it for you. When you are feeling overwhelmed, shout, cry, stomp, and let it out. Don't try to suppress it. The more you try to suppress what is trying to come out, the more the enemy gains a foothold and gains control. After you have released your emotional baggage, turn to God, and He will show you the way to go. Open your heart and allow God to refresh you and fill you up. He will direct your path.

Prayer: Father, help me to understand that you are my light and my strength and I can hold on to you in my weakest moment. When I feel overwhelmed, teach me to meditate on your Word and You will show me the way to go in Jesus' name.

Day 26

Isaiah 43:18 - "Do not call to mind the former things, Or ponder things of the past."

Are you shifting your marketing strategies to align with how you draw individuals to your business as the economy adjusts? When things change, you must be willing to allow your business or ministry to change as well. Many businesses and ministries have closed because they didn't know how to pivot. Don't be stuck in the former way of doing things. Ask God to give you fresh ideas and strategies to grow your business and to reach new demographics. Major retailers who have been in business for years close or go bankrupt because they aren't willing to move in a new direction. What worked for you last year may not work this year, including people who have been with you since the beginning of your business.

When was the last time you evaluated your team? Have they outgrown their current roles? Will they be more useful with other responsibilities? Even the best person on your team needs suggestions and ways to improve. The worst thing you can ever become as a CEO is stagnant. The way you managed your business a few years ago may pose a problem for you this year if you aren't willing to modify or improve your current business tactics. Things change. Businesses change. People change. You change. Change is a sign of growth that challenges the norm or what has become comfort. Change causes conflict and resistance initially, but it's necessary for the sustainability of your company. Clients are attracted to fresh and cutting-edge approaches and employees enjoy working for a company that stands out.

If your business or ministry has reached a plateau, God can revive your business and do new things if you are open to letting go of the old methods to allow Him to give you a revised plan. God is concerned about your business because it can be used as an evangelist tool to draw others to Him; therefore, you should be praying and seeking God regarding your business' daily activities and strategies. He wants you to succeed. He has a vested interest in your business, in you. You are His business; therefore, you must be about His business.

Above all else, God loves you, and His plans are good towards you. He has not brought you this far in your business or ministry without being able to take you further. Let go of the things that have been holding you hostage to the old way of doing things. Let creativity create! Renew your mind. Revive your vision. Rejuvenate your team. Refresh your strategies and measure the outcome. You will be surprised at what a new appeal can do to your business or ministry.

Prayer: Father, I thank you for the fresh wind that is coming to my business and my company's growth. I seek you for creative ideas and marketing strategies. Help me not to be fearful to let go of the things that have not worked and be open to embrace newness in Jesus' name, Amen.

Day 27

> *2 Corinthians 6:14, "Don't team up with those who are unbelievers. How can righteousness be a partner with wickedness? How can light live with darkness?"*

Be careful who you decide to partner or team up with because every person who says, "Lord, Lord," will not enter the Kingdom of Heaven. In other words, those who say that they have your back today have the potential to be the ones who will break your back. It is important that you know those with whom you labor amongst. Get to know their temperament, attitude, skillset, beliefs, and home life by spending time chatting and listening.

As a CEO, you can choose whom you work with; however, the Holy Spirit will give you discernment as to the right people to bring onto your team. This doesn't mean that everybody that you bring to your team has to be like you. As a matter of fact, their expertise should be different from yours. Being sensitive to the Holy Spirit will help you to avoid many mistakes when it comes to choosing people on your team. He will also help you align the vision with the right people.

People will demonstrate their belief system based upon how they handle circumstances and situations in the good and bad times. If you offend the mind, you will reveal the conversations of the heart. When people are upset with you or they don't agree with the decisions you make in your life and business, monitor the actions and conversations of those individuals. Don't say a word; just watch. Their actions will speak louder than their words. It's the same analogy as a job seeker who writes the perfect resume but is unable to perform their duties. Never measure the heart of your team by mere words, but the true motives and thoughts will be revealed during conflict and actions. What the Bible says is true, that out of the abundance of the heart, the mouth speaks.

Don't compromise your integrity for profit or people or jeopardize your core values to avoid conflict. Conflicts will arise in business or ministry. There will always be a difference in opinion. Learn to hear others' point of view even if it differs from yours. Therefore, choose your team wisely and give them permission to think outside the box and think differently from you. Ask them questions and involve them when you have to make decisions. Just because you started the company doesn't mean that your opinion is the only one that matters, as long as it aligns with your core values and morals.

Experiences, skills, and expertise should never trump core values. You can teach a skill, but core values are developed in time. If you've felt as if you are unequally yoked with someone, don't be afraid of confrontation. God will give you wisdom and the words to say to build them up. It is important not to be drawn into the emotional rut that may happen initially because people's first method of operation is to become defensive when confronted.

Confrontation isn't bad. It can lead to growth for everyone involved if managed properly. Your response matters. God will always show you how to say what needs to be said, and He will show you the path to take because you are the light.

Prayer: Father, thank you for choosing the right people for my team. Even if they aren't people that I would normally choose to work with, I trust your judgment.. Help me to lean upon your wisdom and be slow to speak, slow to respond and quick to listen in Jesus' name. Amen.

Day 28

Philippians 2:13 NLT- "For God is working in you, giving you the desire and the power to do what pleases him."

As a CEO, you will go through a time in your life that seems as if everything is going down a different path other than what you've planned. Initially, it may seem negative because it will happen all of a sudden. It's as if things are perfect one minute, then overnight you wake up in a season of chaos that has the ability to stop you dead in your tracks and throw you into a state of depression. It happens to every leader; even the most faith Bible-reading, church-going tither can't avoid the hardships that happen when you're building. The first thing that we sometimes do is remind God how obedient we have been to Him. But obeying God does not exclude you from trials and tribulations. As a matter of fact, according to the Bible, God's faithful followers are the ones who go through the most.

During your process, the enemy will make you feel as if God isn't with you, or he will try to convince you to believe his lies. When Jesus was led into the wilderness by the spirit to be tempted, the devil tried to entice Jesus during the time He was most vulnerable to test His call. The scripture states that the devil said, "If you are the Son of God….." He only said that when Jesus became very weak and hungry. Therefore, you are going to feel persuaded and pressured on every side - and question everything around you, even your purpose in life, especially if the vision isn't aligning or you experience hurt and pain from the people who you have supported the most. This is called your wilderness experience, and God is working on you, giving you power.

I can only imagine how David felt going through ultimate betrayal from someone that he was called to serve. And David had to honor him by not killing him or seeking revenge, even though his leader was trying to kill him. What was God GOD truly doing in David's life to allow him to go through such a rough time in his life? Giving him the desire and power to do what pleases the Lord.

When things happen in your life and it seems as if nothing is going right, it's easy to point fingers or look for an outlet, but what you are encountering has nothing to do with what's around you versus what's happening on the inside of you. This is a necessary part of your success and you can't pray it away. Job was considered blameless, yet He lost everything for the glory of God.

After God allowed Job to go through his season of trauma, he triumphed. It elevated him, and he was restored two times greater than what he lost. Every test is going to lead to elevation. Your increase. Your next level. It's all about you. God uses the wilderness experience to grow, mature, and isolate you for the promise. When Jesus was being tempted, no one was there but the spirit of God. He couldn't be rescued from what he had to go through.

In order for you to see what God has promised you, He has to work on something far greater in you than what you have now, and it seems lonely. It may seem as if you are losing, but these are the moments that really place us at His feet. God has to perform surgery and remove the part of you that has the potential to destroy the blessings that he has in store for you.

Prayer: Father, help me to understand that you are working in me far greater than what I can see today and that the power that will be birthed inside of me after this will help me with the next level of my success. God, I trust you even when I don't understand you. I plant my feet on a solid foundation in which I stand in you, in Jesus' name.

Day 29

Proverbs 29:11 - "Give freely and become more wealthy, be stingy and lose everything."

As a leader, it is important to create opportunities in your company that show it supports great causes, the community, and underprivileged families. It's a great tool to use as a marketing strategy as well. People need to know that you care and you give to causes. The more your business gives, the more you are able to use those moments to help others and attract new clients. Give people a reason to do business with you by combining a cause with a product, and offer additional value without losing out on revenue or compromising the integrity of your brand.

Oftentimes, clients are more likely to support companies that give in different ways. By doing so, it opens up the portals for your business to receive and reach more people. The Bible is true when it says that it is far better to give than receive. However, many struggle with this principle, especially if expenses exceed profits and if it is not part of their lifestyle. Whatever you do in your life, you will duplicate in your business. If you're not good with managing money, then you won't be in your business. If you're not a giver, then your business will not make giving a priority. You may feel that you don't have anything to give, but there is more than one way of giving, such as bartering services, volunteering, supporting other organizations, partnerships, and creating opportunities for giving without having a sale. As a prime example, one restaurant asked us to round up our purchases to the next dollar to support St. Jude. In this scenario, the company doesn't lose money; they just created the opportunity to give. Giving is a great way to build your brand and get others to understand that serving and giving is a core value of your company. And it is definitely a way to honor the Lord.

If you govern your life by giving, it produces wealth for you. Wealth is not money. Wealth is favor and grace that create opportunities to generate money and great success. The opposite of being wealthy is being broke. A broke person can have a lot of money, but without favor and grace, that person will lose everything. Money is not your currency; giving is.

A broke person can have a lot of money, and a wealthy person can have no money but has grace, favor, and connections. You don't have to have all the money in the world as long as you have access to it. Giving will open doors and put you before great men; witty ideas will drop in your spirit, and God will anoint your hands to prosper. He will accelerate you to the front of the line. Give your way to the top, and eventually, you will see what you are willing to give.

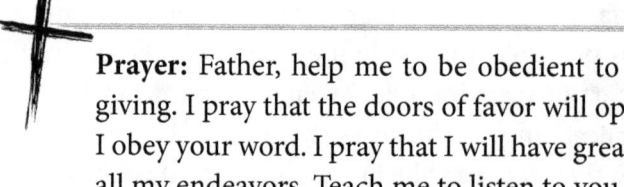

Prayer: Father, help me to be obedient to you in my giving. I pray that the doors of favor will open because I obey your word. I pray that I will have great success in all my endeavors. Teach me to listen to you at all times in Jesus' name. Amen

Day 30

> *1 Peter 4:2 "You won't spend the rest of your lives chasing your own desires, but you will be anxious to do the will of God."*

As a believer, you should be taking time to fast, pray and hear God about your ministry and business venture. It is He who gives wisdom to make it successful. Without the wisdom of God, you will find yourself chasing every money-making opportunity and following your own path and way of thinking. His ways and thoughts are higher than yours; therefore, the way you see your business and your purpose far exceed what God sees and knows about you. That's why God should be able to use any and every part of your life for His glory. He will rearrange your plan, reroute your business, and allow stumbling blocks to knock you off your own course to get you on His.

God does this so that our will aligns with his. When Jesus was in the garden, He told the Father, "not my will but let your will be done." Even Jesus had to get to the point of submission. We are here to carry out God's will. Once Jesus fulfilled his purpose on Earth to pay the wages of our sins, His job here was done.

There is a desire that God has for your business or ministry. He planted it in your life to fulfill your purpose on earth. There are many things you could be doing; just make sure that it aligns with His purpose. God created you with a plan, and when he thought about creating, building, implementing, or tearing down, He said, "let me create _____(insert your name) to operate in this mountain of influence. God has a specific task for you to accomplish here. I believe that every person has a sphere of influence in one of the mountains of influence. The seven mountains of influence are family, religion, education, media, entertainment, business, and government. Which one do you think you're called to operate in? You may have more than one. You may start in one and cross over into another. Once you understand where you belong, you will begin to understand your purpose and gain more clarity on the reason you were born and what you were purposed to do. You will find yourself feeling more anxious and excited to do His will.

One of the reasons why individuals chase their own path is because they are unsure about their purpose. They don't have clarity about their life. You don't have to know all the steps, but you need to be clear in the direction you're going; otherwise you will be chasing your own desires. Imagine driving down the road, not knowing where you are going; where would it lead you? Who knows. There is a difference between driving and not having a destination; versus driving and at least having a destination in mind. If you get lost, you can always use your GPS or ask someone, but when you don't know where you want to go, you will waste money, time, and gas, and no one can help you. It will easily create frustration in your life. Stop chasing your own motives and desires. Slow down, stop if you have to, in order to get clarity, then start again, so you can be anxious to do the will of the Father.

Prayer: Father, help me to take a step back from my agenda to seek your, face regarding the plan of action for my life. Convict me when I am only pursuing my selfish ways and help me to be anxious to do only the will of the Father in Jesus' name!

Day 31

Matthew 6:14-15 NIV "For if you forgive other people when they sin against you, your heavenly Father will also forgive you. But if you do not forgive others their sins, your Father will not forgive your sins.

Everyone makes mistakes, bad choices, and regrettable decisions as a leader. It's part of life. The Bible says that a righteous man falls down, but he gets back up again. Only the righteous get up. What gives a person the ability to get up? Forgiveness. Unforgiveness is like a brick house sitting on top of you, causing you not to be able to move and be productive. All you do is lay there and blame others for what was done to you; rehearsing the act over and over again...bound and limited by pain. Unfortunately, some of the negative actions that have been done against you have been intentional. How you handle the situation will demonstrate whether you are exhibiting the fruit of the spirit or whether you have allowed the enemy to convince you that you have the right to hold on to unforgiveness.

God gave us a command to forgive those who mistreat us, and no matter how bad it hurts, you are accountable to the Most High God. Oftentimes, we feel justified in our actions towards others and more than likely, maybe you should; however, when God is the CEO of your life, He will never allow anything to hurt you or any person to cause you harm without a plan to use it to bring Him glory. Not everything that has happened in your business or ministry by employees, partners, clients, and even with family and friends was God's plan for it to happen, but since it did, He will use it. The key to keeping your heart purified is FORGIVENESS towards others and yourself. When you forgive, you are freeing yourself and releasing God to vindicate on your behalf; however, God chooses to do so is His business and not yours. Sometimes we get upset; because God didn't handle people the way that we wanted him to. God has a plan even for those who have mistreated you. Trust God and let God be God

Unforgiveness is a blessing blocker that stops God from moving freely in your life. You are not in His will when you deliberately choose to hold on to what others have done to you. There are things that have happened in my relationships that I wanted to hold on to, because it seemed as if the person was getting away without punishment, but God said, "Dee that's MY job." It doesn't feel good having to choose to forgive others when you are left with the pain, but when you don't, you can't receive what belongs to you - forgiveness from the Father. God will never do anything contrary to His Word; therefore, sin remains between you and God because He can't forgive you for your sin. You are due the penalty and wages of your sin. You void out what was done on the cross, and now you have to pay the wages for your own sin. You'll pay in business failure, low client retention, financial burden, relationship issues, mental illness, and other attacks from the enemy. Unforgiveness opens the door for the enemy to walk in and set up camp in your life. He has legal access and authority in your life, to your family, your business, or ministry. You can't control where he goes when you let him in, and he can't be removed when he has been granted legal access due to unforgiveness until you forgive.

Imagine a thief having liberty, and free reign in your business or ministry; going through your bank account, taking your vision, spreading rumors, and going into every office doing whatever he wanted. Imagine this thief having residency also in your house. Now he's traveling from your business or ministry to your home. He's everywhere, enjoying everything that belongs to you and wreaking havoc on you and your loved ones. That's the type of access we give the devil when we don't forgive. Check your heart! Who are you refusing to forgive? Forgive, let go, learn, and cut off all demonic access today. Once you have forgiven others, then you will receive the forgiveness of Christ.

Prayer: Father, examine my heart and if there is any place that I am harboring unforgiveness or retaliation towards others, teach me how to trust you and let go so that I may truly receive forgiveness from you in Jesus' name. Amen.

Prophetic Encouragement and Declarations

I pray that this devotional has helped you with being a better ministry or business leader. I pray that you will use these scriptures, examples, and prayers to help you build and lead God's way. May God give you a blueprint for your business or ministry. In order to build whatever God is giving you, the first tool you need is a clear written plan, known as a playbook others can easily interpret. When he received the Ten Commandments, Moses spent time alone with God before he gave the instructions to the Israelites. You too, must receive direction from God before giving your business or ministry commandments to others. If others can't understand the plan, the business will fail. If you are stuck or in disarray, seek the source, then revisit the plan.

Sometimes frustration is a tool that God uses to help us turn back to him. You're learning, so be patient with yourself as you learn the process of building God's way. Yes, you may have seen others do it a certain way, but you have your own learning curve. There is a way that the Lord wants to speak to you. He's raising you up with new creativity, new insights, and new commandments.

Moses went to the mountain twice to receive the full instructions. Each time he received five commandments. Every time you go in the presence of God concerning your business, it should make the previous message from God clearer. Receiving clarity helps you and your team to endure. At this stage, the question shouldn't be whether God called you. Now you should be saying, **"God, since you called me, show me the way."**

You have what it takes; now build it! God has more that He wants to reveal to you. If Moses had only received Five out of the Ten Commandments, what would this world be today? What would have happened if he didn't revisit the mountain to spend time with God? What would have happened if he had allowed the people to make him come up with a decision based on peer pressure? The vision will continue to grow, and oftentimes your frustration will too but don't move until God says so. Wait on God and visit Him often.

It may seem as if you have a vision that is bigger than your resource... one that is bigger than you. Let me reassure you that you do, and it will surely come to pass if you remain diligent. Keep casting the vision to your team, strangers, and whoever will listen, and when they read it or hear it, others will use their favor, resources, and connection on your behalf to help it come to pass. You are anointed for such a time as this. Join me for these decrees.

- I decree and declare that I am the head and not the tail. I am above and not beneath. I am known in the city and in the field.
- I decree that the Lord will make me famous and give me great success.
- I decree that the Lord will establish my name and my works all over the Earth. I will be sought out for my services and my brand.
- I decree that I will be in good health as my soul prospers.

- I decree that I will thrive during a recession. I will not lack. I will not go broke. I will make millions, save millions, tithe millions, invest millions, and give millions. I am a money magnet.
- I decree that the Lord will bless the works of my hand. Everything that I touch shall prosper and succeed.
- I decree that my mind is clear, and I make sound decisions.
- I decree that my business or ministry is thriving, and God is adding to it daily.
- I decree that people from all over the world will do business with me. My clientele increases. My sales increase. My revenue increases. My profit increases.
- I decree that I am not a failure; I am a success. I am the righteousness of Christ, and I will dwell in His House forever.
- I decree that I am not restricted, and there are no boundaries to what God is going to do through my business and ministry.
- I decree I have the best, supportive, loyal, honest, and hardworking team in the world.
- I decree my family loves me and calls me blessed. I have it all. I lack no good thing. God is in everything I do in Jesus' name.